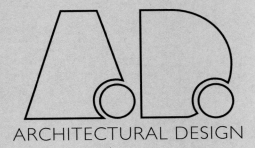

ARCHITECTURAL DESIGN

MW01015887

EDITORIAL OFFICES:
42 LEINSTER GARDENS, LONDON W2 3AN
TEL: + 44 71 402 2141 FAX: + 44 171 723 9540

GUEST EDITOR: Charles Jencks
EDITOR: Maggie Toy
PRODUCTION EDITOR: Ellie Duffy
ART EDITOR: Alex Young

CONSULTANTS: Catherine Cooke, Terry Farrell, Kenneth Frampton, Charles Jencks, Heinrich Klotz, Leon Krier, Robert Maxwell, Demetri Porphyrios, Kenneth Powell, Colin Rowe, Derek Walker

SUBSCRIPTION OFFICES:

UK: JOHN WILEY & SONS LTD
JOURNALS ADMINISTRATION DEPARTMENT
1 OAKLANDS WAY, BOGNOR REGIS
WEST SUSSEX, PO22 9SA, UK
TEL: 01243 843272 FAX: 01243 843232
E-mail:cs-journals@wiley.co.uk

USA AND CANADA:
JOHN WILEY & SONS, INC
JOURNALS ADMINISTRATION DEPARTMENT
605 THIRD AVENUE
NEW YORK, NY 10158
TEL: + 1 212 850 6645 FAX: + 1 212 850 6021
CABLE JONWILE TELEX: 12-7063
E-mail: subinfo@wiley.com

ALL OTHER COUNTRIES:
WILEY-VCH GmbH
POSTFACH 101161
69451 WEINHEIM
FEDERAL REPUBLIC OF GERMANY
TEL: + 49 6201 606 148 FAX: + 49 6201 606 184

Subscription rates for 1997 (incl p&p): Annual subscription price: UK only £74.00, World DM 195 for regular subscribers. Student rate: UK only £53.00, World DM 156 incl postage and handling charges. Individual issues: £18.95/DM 45.00 (plus £2.30/DM 5 for p&p, per issue ordered).
For the USA and Canada: Architectural Design is published six times per year (Jan/Feb; Mar/Apr; May/Jun; Jul/Aug; Sept/Oct; and Nov/Dec) by Academy Group Ltd, 42 Leinster Gardens, London W2 3AN, England, and distributed by John Wiley & Sons, Inc, Journals Administration Department, 605 Third Avenue, New York, NY 10158, USA. Annual subscription price; US $142.00 including postage and handling charges; special student rates available at $105.00, single issue $29.95. Periodicals postage paid at Jamaica, NY 11431. Air freight and mailing in the USA by Publications Expediting Services Inc, 200 Meacham Ave, Elmont, NY 11003: Send address changes to: 'title', c/o Publications Expediting Services Inc, 200 Meacham Ave, Elmont, NY 11003. Printed in Italy. All prices are subject to change without notice. [ISSN: 0003-8504]

CONTENTS

ARCHITECTURAL DESIGN **MAGAZINE**

Aronoff Center for Design and Art David Gosling
• *Academy Highlights* • *Reviews* • *Books*

ARCHITECTURAL DESIGN **PROFILE** No 129

NEW SCIENCE = NEW ARCHITECTURE?

Charles Jencks *Nonlinear Architecture* •
Eisenman Architects *Aronoff Center for Design and Art* • **Frank O Gehry** *The Guggenheim Museum* • **Ashton Raggatt McDougall** *Storey Hall* • **Mae-Wan Ho** *The New Age of the Organism* • **Peter T Saunders** *Nonlinearity* • **Daniel Libeskind** *The V&A Boilerhouse Extension* • **Foreign Office Architects** *Yokohama International Port Terminal* • **Michael Batty and Paul Longley** *The Fractal City* • **Van Berkel & Bos** *Erasmus Bridge* • **Cecil Balmond** *New Structure and the Informal*

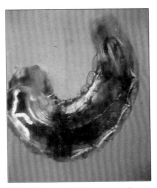

Liquid crystalline organism

Ushida-Finlay Partnership, Truss Wall House, Tokyo

EISENMAN ARCHITECTS

ARONOFF CENTER FOR DESIGN AND ART
UNIVERSITY OF CINCINNATI
David Gosling

This is a brilliant design in many ways. Like all iconoclastic architecture, it is not without its contradictions and aberrations, although most of these were beyond the control of the designer. The University of Cincinnati is a large, midwestern university with some 35,000 students. Founded in 1815, it is an urban university on a 212-acre campus, three miles from the city centre. Its explosive growth during the 1960s led to the building of some of the unsightly architecture of that decade.

In the mid-1980s, the University embarked on a brave, visionary (though highly controversial) further development of the campus. Although journalistic terms like 'signature architects' or 'windows of opportunity' are repugnant to this writer, the new policy of the University administration engaged the services of the best of American architects. It may be argued that an essentially 60s campus (although the 19th-century buildings are elegant) could not be welded together to form a coherent whole. Such is the problem of many British universities, yet the European idea of the American university campus is of manicured lawns, mature trees and a feeling of arcadia epitomised in the campuses of Harvard or Yale. It could be argued that the architecture of Eisenman or Gehry would do little to bring together such a disparate urban sprawl but the opposite was, in fact, the case.

Perhaps one great architect should have been invited to design the whole of the university campus, like Maki at Keio University in Japan or Isozaki at Bond University in Australia, or even Thomas Jefferson at the University of Virginia. However, these were built on virgin sites. Instead, in 1991, George Hargreaves, the San Francisco landscape architect, was invited to prepare a campus 'masterplan' – something of a misnomer since it is really a comprehensive landscape design. Michael Graves' design of the College of Engineering Research Centre is one of powerful architectural imagery and is a surprisingly contextual success. The campus power plant was designed by the Cambridge Seven; the Sigma Sigma tower by Machado and Silvetti, who are also designing the new student halls of residence; the Swing building (constructed as overflow accommodation whilst other structures were being built) by David Childs of Skidmore, Owings and Merrill; the outdoor spectator terrace and plaza by Wes Jones; the Molecular Sciences Institute by Frank Gehry, and Pei, Cobb, Freed have designed extensions to the nationally renowned College Conservatory of Music. All bring together spectacular aspects of late 20th-century architecture.

Peter Eisenman's design was for the addition to the College of Design, Architecture, Art and Planning (henceforth referred to as DAAP). The College had three linked, existing buildings of some 16,000 square metres, and Eisenman's brief was to double the size. The DAAP has approximately 1,750 undergraduates and graduate students and approximately 120 full-time and part-time members of the teaching faculty. Eisenman began his design in August 1987 and the building opened in October 1996. The delays and cost overruns were not overlooked by the press but one has to realise that the teaching staff represent not only architecture, interior design, urban planning and fine art departments but also industrial design, graphic design, fashion design and art history. The DAAP could and should have been the Bauhaus of the late 20th century but like universities throughout the world, there were always internecine rivalries between the factions who argued at length about the internal planning. The object of the university administration was to bring these factions and their students together within the new building and in the first months of its use, this seems to be succeeding.

Eisenman himself performed in an exemplary way. From the very beginning, he visited the campus at monthly intervals to present his designs not only to the entire college (always to a packed house) but to the University Building Design Review Committee and the University Board of Trustees.

Attention was first drawn to his design when he won the *Progressive Architecture* Award in January 1991.[1] Eisenman describes his design thus:

> [Located] on the north side of the existing college, three structures end to end in chevron pattern stand at the top of a knoll sloping east. Library, administration offices, auditorium, photo lab, café and additional studios, laboratories and others together with multi-purposes spaces for juries and exhibits.' The solution: 'the building was conceived as a symbol of the new cosmology of man and information. Just as information comes to us in the media in a fragmented, ambiguous manner, so does this building arise out of a series of formal transformations that fracture and blur traditional architectural dichotomies such as old and new, inside and outside, structure and infill. The form of this architecture school addition takes its cue from the chevron shape of the re-existing building. [We] torqued, tilted and shifted this shape out of phase, resulting in an architecture that carries within its plans and elevations the trace of these formal moves like the after-image on a television screen or the interpenetration of radio frequencies. The chevron shape finally becomes so fuzzy that it takes on the undulating quality of the site. Captured between the space between the new building and the old is a complex skylighted atrium. Walkways and bridges overlook this public space.

It is interesting to note the jury's response. Adele Santos commented:

> Its response to the sloping site is really quite nice. It also has some very fine sections. I think the way the light will come filtering down into the walkways will be very beautiful. What astounds me is that a school of architecture would pick an architect whose work is going to be so clearly defined at a point in time, knowing that would be the image of the school forevermore. This is precisely one of the building types that requires a certain type of neutrality,

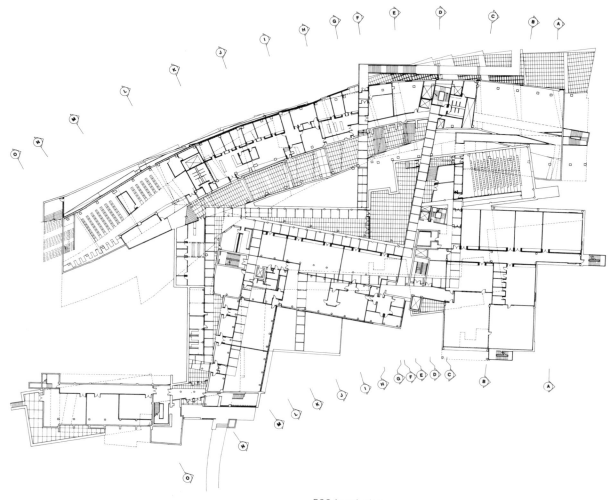

500 level plan

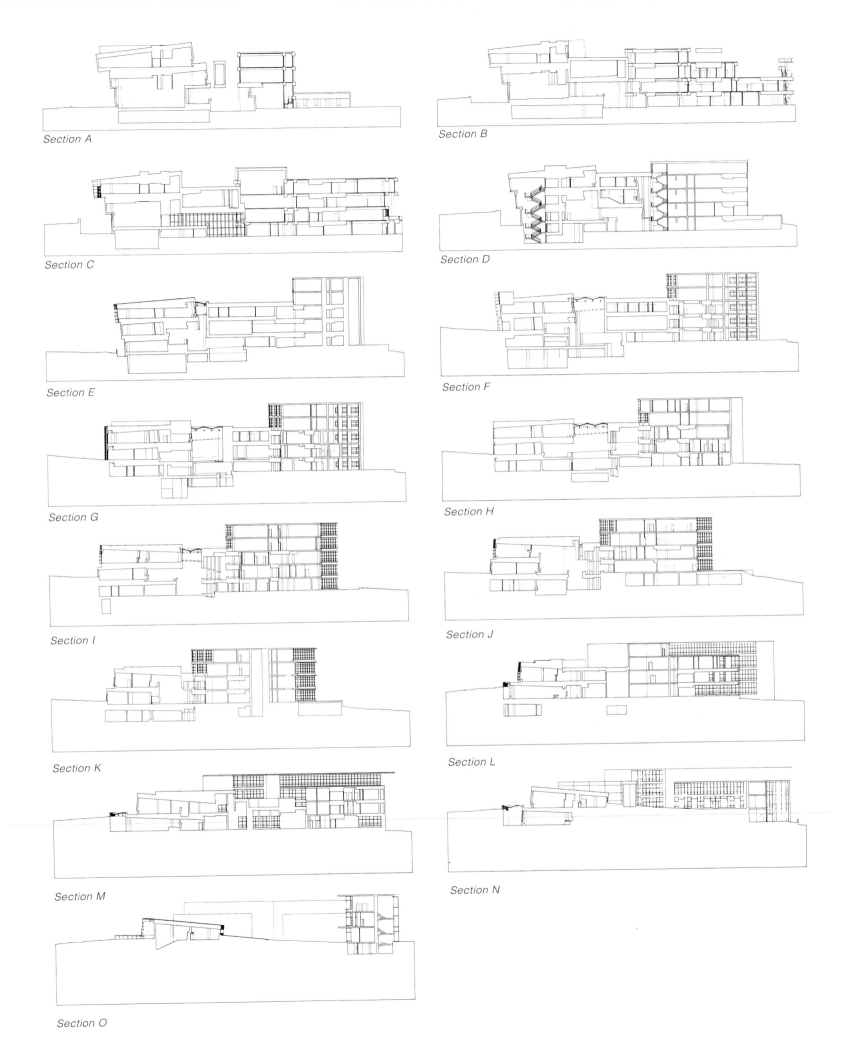

Section A

Section B

Section C

Section D

Section E

Section F

Section G

Section H

Section I

Section J

Section K

Section L

Section M

Section N

Section O

flexibility and open-endedness. This is an enormously particular and highly personal statement.

Ralph Johnson agreed, stating: 'That is true. Architecture schools do tend towards more neutral types of spaces.' (This comment is hardly true in the context of Louis Kahn's Art Gallery and School of Fine Art or Paul Rudolph's School of Architecture, both built at Yale University in the middle of this century.)

Rem Koolhaas continued: 'Yes, but this building is quite clever in terms of organising the utilitarian parts in a utilitarian way. Only with the public spaces does it become expressive', a comment concurred by Dana Cuff: 'The existing buildings are pretty awful.' Ralph Johnson asserted: 'It has an extremely skilful definition of the public spaces and a beautiful treatment of the public corridor.'

What is most remarkable about the design drawings shown in the issue of *Progressive Architecture* in September, 1991 is that the final built form, externally and especially internally, is astonishingly faithful. Rarely has any radical architect achieved this and one can only think of the extreme tenacity of Frank Lloyd Wright on a comparative basis.

When Peter Eisenman first began the design of this building, there was commentary on his work in general in a special edition on Deconstruction Theory in *Architectural Design*.[2] Andrew Benjamin suggests that in examining the architectural metaphor in Descartes,[3] a series of oppositions has emerged in creating a structural role within this philosophical position – he further suggests that it is in relation to these oppositions that the force of Deconstruction can be located. Jacques Derrida suggests that in Deconstruction, analyses and comparative conceptual pairs which are currently accepted as self-evident and natural, appear as if they had not been institutionalised at some precise point, as if they had no history. Derrida considers the work of Tschumi in his plan of the Parc de la Villette in Paris,[4] especially the series of constructs known as 'Les Folies', an architectural expression commonly mis-used in the 19th century. Derrida makes the point that they are not 'madness' (*la folie*). He suggests that despite appearance, Deconstruction is not in itself an architectural metaphor. Benjamin further suggests that 'the challenge presented by Deconstruction is the same challenge it presents to all the arts, as well as philosophy, literary criticism (linguistic theory?) and so forth. It is a challenge that initially takes place on the level of thinking – here in the example of architecture. Thinking becomes enacted in the architectural work of both Eisenman and Tschumi.'

Charles Jencks refers to Eisenman as the 'positive nihilist',[5] suggesting that the latter became a disciple of Deconstruction at the same time as he was undergoing personal trauma and psychoanalysis. He was a member of the New York Five (Eisenman, Gehry, Graves, Gwathmey, Hejduk) in the 1970s and the founder of the Institute for Architecture and Urban Studies in New York City which reached its zenith in 1976-78, closing in 1984. These facts are pertinent in a special way. The jewel-like villas built by the New York Five owed much to neo-Corbusian philosophy and, to a lesser extent, to Terragni. Eisenman's earlier house designs such as House I (Princeton, New Jersey, 1967), House II (Hardwick, Vermont, 1970), House III (Lakeville, Connecticut, 1971) and House IV (Cornwall, Connecticut, 1975) were not really precursors of his later exuberance displayed in the much larger Deconstructionist buildings in Ohio (the Wexner Center for the Visual Arts 1983-89), the Greater Columbus Convention Center (1989-93) and the University of Cincinnati DAAP building (1988-96). The villas explored rectilinear spatial sequences and

interpenetrating volumes and planes with consummate skill. Although House III showed a distinct shift in complexity and contradiction, deliberately lacking the apparent serenity of the other houses, it, perhaps, in 1971, foreshadowed Eisenman's major change in direction. Later, theoretical house studies such as the Fin d'ou T Hous S in 1984 for the Venice Cannaregio Project, or House X, displayed, albeit through orthogonal grids, a different form of complexity.[6]

Philip Johnson selected two American architects for the Fifth International Exhibition of Architecture at the Venice Biennale in 1991, organised by Francesco Dal Co.[7] The two were chosen as architects who were challenging their discipline in an aggressive way and challenging dogma above all else. Johnson suggested that there were, however, great differences in their personalities: Eisenman as the East Coast intellectual and Gehry as an intuitive, anti-intellectual West Coast savant. Eisenman's key display at the Biennale was the design drawings for DAAP.

And yet, for all the praise showered upon Eisenman as the leader of Deconstruction Theory and its architectural application, far less is known about his formidable talents as urban designer. Charles Jencks says in his book, *The Architecture of the Jumping Universe*[8] that no one has looked at the lessons of emerging sciences more strenuously than Eisenman.

Jencks suggests that Peter Eisenman's shift to the non-linear sciences and the new urbanism began in 1987, as with his Rebstock Housing Project in Frankfurt, making extensive use of the 'fold'. In Cincinnati, he introduced the wave form as a transformation of the 'zig-zag' rectangles of the three existing buildings. The Frankfurt Rebstock park has been referred to by Jencks as a shift to the non-linear sciences and a 'new urbanism'. Yet this terminology is confusing because 'The New Urbanism' eloquently explained in a book by Peter Katz[9] and currently sweeping the United States, is generated in part by the forces of conservatism and reaction. 'Seaside' by Andres Duany and Elizabeth Plater-Zyberk, for all its romanticism and elegance, has little to do with urban exploration or 'real' communities for that matter. Eisenman, on the other hand, explored ways of developing new communities of social housing on a major scale, carried out in collaboration with Albert Speer & Partner (Germany) and landscape architects Hanna/Olin in Philadelphia, PA. The findings were published in 1992.[10] The site is a vast tract of land to the north of major railroad marshalling yards. The plan, starting with orthogonal grids, transformed subsequently into warped folds and twisted grids or torques, the initial studies showing a mixture of low-rise and medium-rise housing.

These observations on the Frankfurt project are relevant in view of this critic since the DAAP is essentially more about urban design, both within (with great success) and without (with somewhat lesser success) than it is about a single building or even a group of buildings.

The professional press was generally euphoric about the new building; the local press less so. The *Cincinnati Enquirer*, in an editorial of 2 February, 1997, stated:

> The University President said that $71.4 million had been cut from UC's budget in the last decade . . . But rather than see that as falling bad sky news, we think his fiscal responsibility is good news. And so is UC's campus where new buildings . . . seem to grow faster than Magic Rocks. The aim of today's comparison photos is not to disparage UC or suggest that University classrooms should be as shabby and dilapidated as many of our elementary schools.

Benjamin Forey, writing in the *Washington Post*, said that although Eisenman is not great in the way that Frank Lloyd Wright and Le Corbusier were, who changed architectural direction fundamentally, Eisenman's design emphasises the importance of 'route' which neither of the two great 20th-century masters confronted. Forey believed that the design was intended to be a polemical statement – sometimes to invigorate, sometimes to annoy. An open-closed-open spatial sequence clothed in unconventional forms, intended to heighten surprise and pleasure, snakes up the hill; the more conventional spaces, such as the classrooms, library and offices, tended to be left over spaces – little nooks and crannies. He thought that 'Eisenman identified himself as a radical avant-gardist, critical of mainstream architecture'. Yet Eisenman's Convention Center in Ohio's state capital, Columbus, is a totally mainstream building as he suggested; however, the Wexner Center at Ohio State University in Columbus is not. Forey commented on Eisenman's sources – archaeological excavations, a fascination shared with Hargreaves (the triangulated 'Indian Burial Mounds' are an integral part of the DAAP design), mathematical models, the Boolian cube used in computer modelling, chemical compounds such as DNA, geometrical conundrums and philosophies as diverse as Noam Chomsky and Jacques Derrida.

Each of the three Ohio buildings are quite different. DAAP is his first truly curvilinear building of brick, glass and steel with dramatic grids, diagonal lines and towers – together with lay-lines or lines of force of the Druids (which Hargreaves in his landscape design for the University of Cincinnati refers to as the 'braids'). The Columbus Convention Center is a big box deliberately fragmented with a startling array of abstract forms. The DAAP building, Forey commented, was externally curiously modest and reticent.

Due to the wishes of the University administration the knoll upon which the DAAP is sited was not reduced in height, as Eisenman originally wished. This is quite tragic since half the height of Eisenman's building is hidden behind berms and grass mounds. Pastel pinks, greens and blues are used. Again, as in earlier designs, Eisenman wanted to use much bolder colours; again, he demurred to the University's wishes but a look at the *Casabella* appraisal by Kurt Forster[11] reveals how it could have been, through the use of skilful printing techniques. The juxtaposition of the harsh 1960s concrete and mechanical stacks of the Wolfson building at the eastern end of the campus is unfortunate and should have been screened. Their existence was referred to as 'value engineering' – better known as cost cutting. The ridiculous bright yellow parking kiosk was obviously erected without consultation with Eisenman. The internal signage throughout the building is a debased form of Roman typography on brown plates, and raises the question, 'who selected it?' (certainly not Eisenman). These petulant thoughts are raised here only because, given a radical design of such quality, why spoil it with badly considered extras? Other questions arise about the use of external materials such as Dryvit which is a 2.5cm-7cm styrofoam panel with (in European terms) painted cement render.

Forster suggests the total design is like 'a gently orchestrated earthquake'. The building, Eisenman suggests, is like 'the plates of an armadillo or the segments of an airport baggage carousel'.

Paul Goldberger, writing in the *New York Times*, suggests that Eisenman treats this as the most important event in American architecture since Frank Lloyd Wright was able to convince Solomon Guggenheim that pictures look good in round spaces.

Philip Johnson announced that it has 'no equal in American architecture'. Goldberger describes it thus: 'Few walls are perpendicular; three bland institutional buildings are joined together, frozen after the first shocks of an earthquake. (There is a sense of vertigo and seasickness in some of the spaces.)'[12] Is this, Goldberger asks, the final gasp of modernism and the beginning of something else? Was it just intended to grab attention? The breaking of barriers between inside and outside, the blurring of form and function? These questions can only be answered by studying Peter Eisenman's design process.

In an elegant, limited edition book edited by Cynthia Davidson, *Eleven Authors in Search of a Building*, one of the essays by Donna Barry (a key project architect) explains this succinctly. Barry and Michael McInturf, the project site architect, offer a great insight into this process: Eisenman is not the director of a huge practice which delegates design. Like Frank Lloyd Wright, he *is* the designer. Nevertheless, as Wright influenced the impressive architecture of Fay Jones, his former apprentice, McInturf, who is now on the teaching faculty of the School of Architecture, won a 1997 *Progressive Architecture* Award in his own right, and is a member of the Senior Year Thesis studio team under the leadership of David Niland. Donna Barry summarises the design process as follows:

> The strategy was to react to the fundamental rules of construction while creating a space that appears to contradict or ignore them. For example, in science the process of symmetry breaking explains observed complexity within a non-linear system. Space can be curved, mass is not constant and the relative position of the body affects the measurement of the space between the object and the body.
>
> The building represents a process of symmetry breaking in the design process of the building, providing a new awareness of the human experience in space by disrupting the conventional relationships between form, function and meaning. The idea of self-similarity is an example of a process analogous to symmetry breaking. Self-similarity is a process of repetition that produces an asymmetry. Self-similarity sets up a duality between the original form and the copy or trace of that form. The original and the trace are then superimposed to create a third form that incorporates them both.
>
> The resulting design is based on a dynamic mathematically non-linear design process. The series of displacements attempt to redefine the human experience of space.
>
> **Step 1**: A series of three-dimensional rectangles creating the juxtaposition of studio, corridor and office (each rectangle approximately 13 metres x 21 metres). The height of the box is the floor-to-floor height of approximately 4.8 metres.
>
> **Step 2**: The line was transformed into a curve to contrast with the hard rectilinear edge of the three existing buildings. The curved line was made complex in both plan and section. Graphically, such a curved line describes a non-linear, mathematical relationship. The line was transformed into the construction of a curve without a centre.
>
> **Step 3**: The transformation of the segmented line into a curve and the box geometry was overlapped horizontally, based on a logarithmic function. In the non-linear nature of the relationship between the boxes, the algorithm that produced this logarithmic function was developed so that no overlap would be sequentially repeated.

Step 4: Another algorithm was derived simultaneously with the overlap to introduce a tilt or twist to each box in the x-y axis. The algorithm produced the twist applied to a particular box. The asymptotic curve is generated out of the two systems such that this lack of relationship between the two systems reinforces the idea that nothing in the lines is constant or predictable. The resulting conditions are neither regular nor random; nor are they an example of individual expressionism or related to any historical iconography.

Step 5: In order to locate the diagram in section, a relationship between the box and the floor slab had to be determined, certainly as a practical response to the reality of construction. The dimension of this relationship was required to be approximately one metre, measured from the north bottom of the box along the axis. Each box was torqued independently along the z axis while changing direction along the x-y axis. There was a resulting relationship between the horizontal datum and the torqued box, allowing a consistent reading between the two elements. This set of overlapped, twisted and torqued boxes is referred to as a phase. In physics, phase transitions refer to the behaviour of matter near the point where it changes from one state into another, from a liquid to a gas, or from magnetised to unmagnetised.

Step 6: The original geometric phase is shifted twice along the x axis in order to produce a series of three phases for each functional level (levels 400, 500 and 600). Each phase maintains the form of the original x-y twist. The applied torque to each box of each phase varies at each level, so there is no one-to-one relationship possible in section. The uppermost 600 level has the most extreme torque, while the lower 400 level has the least torque. This series of torques is descriptively referred to as the torqued solid series.

Step 7: The torqued solid series is shifted and copied along the x-y axis and dropped in elevation as a complete series. This lowering in the x plane purposely blurs the section while the shift in the y plane blurs the plan. This series of phases traced over the torqued solid series is referred to as the torqued trace series. The original phase is copied to form a self-similar series. This series is then copied to form a self-similar trace. These two series create an overlapped figure that became programmatically the atrium space of the building.

Step 8: The diagrams could not merely be placed level on the site. The east edge of the site became the 200 or mechanical level of the building while the west edge climbs to an elevation referred to as the 600 level. This creates the need to walk not only through but up the building. The stepping phase takes the same form as the initial phase but with three distinct differences. The height of each box totals the three levels – approximately 14 metres and each box steps consecutively in elevation. Each box is vertical without a torque along the z axis. This distinguishes the stepping boxes from the torquing boxes so that one can be read against the other. Finally, these two series are shifted in plan, necessary to provide the notation for stepping 'on and up' the slope. The stepping series that takes the form of the original phase is referred to as the stepping solid series, while the shifted image of this phase is referred to as its trace.

Step 9: The figure created by the overlapping torqued solid

Jeff Goldberg/Esto

Jeff Goldberg/Esto

Jeff Goldberg/Esto

series and torqued trace series of boxes defines the space of what is called the atrium or 'College Hall'. This third element is created by the superimposition of the solid form and trace form. It is a negative space produced from the overlapped condition. It becomes a path that traverses the sectional contours of the site notated by the stepping series. Beginning at ground level as an exterior element of the east 200 level garage, the atrium space ascends through a series of platforms to the 400 level entry and forms the main interior, the central space. This negative space continues to rise through yet another series of platforms used as critique areas for all the four schools to the 500 level. At the entry to the library in the west segment, the negative space rises again to the 600 level and exists to the west at the top of the hill with a cascade of stairs down to Clifton Avenue. In the case of the existing three buildings, each is separated by a stair tower. The addition has independent floor levels and the 500 level of the new building is the only common level for all four buildings.

The three-metre wide corridor in the original DAAP is described as a chevron, used to extend a similar figure across the site. The northern chevron refers to the Alms trace. The southern chevron is referred to as the Wolfson Building trace. The composite in these traces creates a blur between the original and the trace. The chevron zone is defined as the space between two chevron figures. The portion of a box edge that passes through any chevron remains in its original location. Just as the existing building traces blur, in plan, the edges of the existing building, the chevron figures blur the edges of the box geometry. The combination of interlocking boxes and traces is reminiscent of the moving facets of an airport baggage carousel.

Step 10: The structural 'grid' is organised by the 500 level torqued solid phase of boxes. As a result, the rectilinear column grid moves through the space, independent of the form of that space. Columns pass in, out and through the walls. Vertical on one side and sloped with the building's geometry on the other, these columns read against the round columns that are part of the trace of existing buildings. Some columns are not structural – in some cases, they are part of a figure traced from the existing buildings, contradicting the notion of the structural column.

Step 11: The examination of space in the third dimension afforded by the computer creates a problem for construction that is based on the convention of planar extrusion. The programming and planning of functions were organised, and a form evolved from *within* the three-dimensional wire frame provided by the computer. The space of the building was not conceived a priority but rather emerged from the process of design. The conventional building section is incapable of providing the information required to build this form, in part because it is not possible to draw a meaningful section of the building since it would be orthogonal to only one box in the wire frame.

The co-ordinate system typically used in surveying was introduced as a method for dimensioning this project. Conventional string dimensions on the floor plans were not useful to locate each box edge in reference to the column grid and Euclidean measurements of length depth and thickness. Ideas of longitude, latitude and altitude were better suited to the twisted and the torqued geometry of this project. A benchmark was located at the northwest corner of the old Alms building. The edge of each box was located in relation to this control mark in x-y-z co-ordinates. Co-ordinate points were assigned at the intersection of the floor slab and the interlocked edges of the torqued walls. The contractors used a laser transit method of triangulation to locate points on lines and to calculate distances between co-ordinate points. The staked points were connected by lasers to lay out the track for studwalls and ceilings. The co-ordinate plans are like 'join-the-dot drawings' but without numbers. The contractor was able to 'join these dots' without prior knowledge of the object to be drawn.

Step 12: Conceptual transformations and the construction drawings do not describe the space of the building. Drawings can only depict the form, of which the oneric space is the result . . . the logic remains elusive. This intrinsic logic is not intended to be read easily by the building's viewer or user.' Donna Barry concludes her analysis thus: 'The space of this project has a labyrinthine quality. It is experienced as a logical but not easily read path: a discovered path'.[13]

Cynthia Davidson refers to Colin Rowe's *Promenade Architecturale*,[14] suggesting that as the building climbs a hill, a route, giving continuously unfolding views, talks of chevrons, x-y-z co-ordinates, asymptotic tilts and torquing. No facade. The entry at 300 level reveals no promenade architecturale and there is re-entry at the 400 level.

However, this is what the design is all about and analogies with the theories of Gordon Cullen's 'serial vision' and Frank Lloyd Wright's 'organic architecture' and the Usonian House seem to be pertinent. It is unlikely that all three, Wright, Cullen and Eisenman, would agree with this!

Gordon Cullen suggested that the perception of the town as a piece of moving scenery hardly enters the head of the person in the street, yet, this is usually what the town is – a moving set. Cullen showed this in a remarkably evocative way, illustrating an uninterrupted sequence of views which would unfold themselves like 'stills' from a movie.[15]

Many theorists of the Modern Movement[16] included two important concepts which came together in the 1920s and which are relevant to urban designers. The first of these, with origins in De Stijl painting and the architecture of Frank Lloyd Wright, was the concept of space as a natural continuum, with no distinction between external and internal spaces. Both Sigfried Giedion's 'space time' and Moholy Nagy's 'Vision in Motion' drew attention to a more dynamic approach to visual understanding which seemed to offer new insights into the processes of describing and analysing urban environments. The distinction between this appreciation based upon a mobile observer and the former perception from static, frontal viewpoints was similarly developed by other commentators such as those of Roger Hinks.[17] Similarly, Arata Isozaki has maintained that the Japanese do not recognise the Western concept of space and time.[18] Both are, rather, conceived in Japanese terms of intervals, as reflected in the use of the term 'Ma' in architecture, landscape design, music and drama, a concept which can signify the 'natural distance' between two or more objects existing in a continuity.

Peter Eisenman's DAAP building is a lesson in space-time. It is an enigma. Modest on the exterior, half-buried in the hillside landscape, it reveals little of its dazzling interior. In seeding analogies with Frank Lloyd Wright, America's greatest organic architect says:

Plasticity was a familiar term, but something I had seen in no buildings whatsoever . . . You may see the appearance of the thing in the surface of your hand as contrasted with the articulation of the bony skeleton itself. This ideal, profound in its architectural implications, soon took on another conscious stride forward in a new aesthetic. I called it continuity (it is easy to see it as a *folded plane*). Continuity in this aesthetic sense appeared to me as the natural means to achieve truly organic architecture . . . [19]

Externally, Eisenman's design, in its sinuous curvilinear way, exemplifies in its relationship to the hillside everything that was true about Wright's organic architecture. It grows out of, and is part of the landscape. It is surprisingly reticent. And yet, the only point of the building which is separated from its predecessor, is the northwest corner (ignored by architectural photographers). It is the one point where 'serial vision', 'space time' and sequential spaces between inside and outside come into play. It is separated at this point from the chevron of the three existing buildings. It is almost perfect in itself. Yet, all of the external building is mostly north-facing where sunlight can play little part in enhancing the articulation of the elements. Some of the beautiful black leather and white steel furniture by Knoll in public spaces could well have been sacrificed for floodlighting this building at night. Even without this, the illuminated interior of the 500 level library with its great beams and its uplighting at night is magical to behold.

However, the real magic of this building is its interior public space. It is one of the rare occasions in contemporary design where 'serial vision' as urban design concept comes into play. The continuous cascade of stairs and platforms from the 300 level at the eastern end to the 600 level at the western end is breathtaking. It does not end at street level as other critics have suggested but 12 metres above it. The contrast between the Wexner Center and DAAP is interesting. The Wexner Center has been criticised elsewhere for its exuberant architecture internally. As an art gallery, one should expect it to be reticent like the admirable Van Gogh Museum in Amsterdam but as a piece of urban design with its delicate white pergolas-cum-arcade-cum-colonnade welding together disparate pieces of academic architecture spanning a century, it is a stroke of genius. Externally, DAAP has no such pyrotechnics. It is certainly not contextual, although the urban context is mediocre.

Internally, the spatial experience of ascending (or descending) from level 300 to 600 is breathtaking. At the 400 level, the atrium breaks into a public space, gathering ground, social meeting place, café and party space, fulfilling the requirement of bringing the schools of the College together. It is interesting that most of the architectural photographers, following the example of their Japanese peers, show no people in their photographs. Yet the DAAP atrium is a rare contradiction – at one of the opening celebrations, the atrium was packed with people and it looked marvellous; it needed to be populated, as I am sure Peter Eisenman intended. Its Piranesi-like qualities, with its soaring criss-cross bridges and overlook galleries make it a procession, a 'promenade architecturale', a 'serial vision', a 'space time' experience to be treasured. It is an internal masterpiece.

David Gosling is the State of Ohio Eminent Scholar in Urban Design and Professor of Urban Design at the University of Cincinnati, USA. He is also the author of Gordon Cullen: Visions of Urban Design, *Academy Editions, 1996, which received an American Institute of Architects Award for Architectural Advancement in November 1996.*

The author wishes to acknowledge the assistance of Erica Stoller (Esto photography), Juliette Cezzar of Eisenman Architects and Cynthia Davidson, editor of *Eleven Authors in Search of a Building.*

Notes

1   *Progressive Architecture* 01-09, Progressive Architecture Awards, 1991, pp82-83.
2   Editorial, p7 and pp8-11, Andrew Benjamin, *Architectural Design*, Vol 158, No 314, 1988.
3   Descartes, R, 'Discourse on Method', *The Philosophical Writings of Descartes*, Vol 1, Cambridge University Press (Cambridge),1985.
4   Derrida, J, 'Architetture ove i' desiderio può arbitare', *Domus*, No 671, April 1986.
5   Jencks, C, *Architectural Design*, Vol 158, No 314, 1988, pp26-31 and 49-61.
6   Eisenman, P, *House of Cards*, Oxford University Press (Oxford and New York), 1987.
7   *Architectural Design*, Vol 162, No 1/2, 1992.
8   Jencks, C, *The Architecture of the Jumping Universe*, Academy Editions (London), 1995.
9   Katz, P, *The New Urbanism*, McGraw Hill (New York), 1994.
10 Eisenman et al, *Frankfurt Rebstockpark: Folding in Time*, Prestel-Verlag (Munich) and Deutches Architektur Museum (Frankfurt), 1992.
11 Forster, K, *Casabella*, No 638, October 1996, pp12-16.
12 Goldberger, P, *New York Times*, Monday 14 October 1996, ppB-1 and B-5.
13 Davidson, C (ed), *Eleven Authors in Search of a Building*, Monacelli Press, Inc. (New York), 1996, pp48-95 (Donna Barry).
14 *Ibid*, p14.
15 Gosling, D, *Gordon Cullen: Visions of Urban Design*, Academy Editions (London), 1996, p24.
16 Gosling, D, and B Maitland, *Concepts of Urban Design*, Academy Editions (London), 1984, pp42-43.
17 Hinks, R, 'Peepshow and the Roving Eye', *Architectural Review*, August 1995.
18 *Japan Architect*, February 1979.
19 Frank Lloyd Wright, *The National House*, Horizon Press, 1954, 1982, p18.

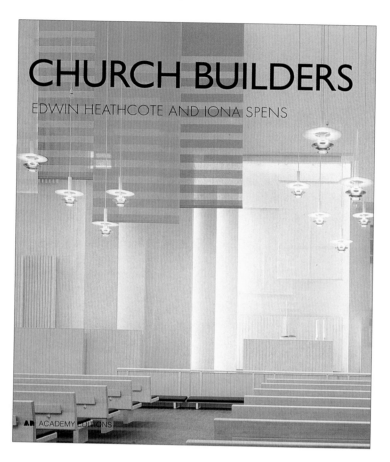

CHURCH BUILDERS

Edwin Heathcote and Iona Spens

Church Builders traces developments in church building through the momentous changes in architecture and theology in the late 19th and 20th centuries, and illustrates the broad spectrum of modern ecclesiastical architecture which has emerged as the synthesis of the pluralism which defined the turn of the century and the purity and clarity of the Modern Movement. Among the many architects featured are Auguste Perret, Rudolf Schwarz, Otto Bartning, Dominikus Böhm, Antoni Gaudí, Frank Lloyd Wright, Le Corbusier, Tadao Ando, Siren Architects, Fay Jones, Philip Johnson, Mario Botta, Imre Makovecz and Juha Leiviskä. This is the fourth title in the successful 'Builders' series. Other titles in this series include *Museum Builders* (1 85490 191 5), *Theatre Builders* (1 85490 450 7) and the recently published *Library Builders* (1 85490 484 1).

Edwin Heathcote is an architect and writer working in London, and is on the editorial staff of *Church Building* magazine. Iona Spens is an architectural historian and writer who lives and works in London.

HB, 0 471 97755 1, 305 x 252 mm, 224 pages. Illustrated throughout, mainly in colour. £45.00 $75.00 DM147.00: October 1997

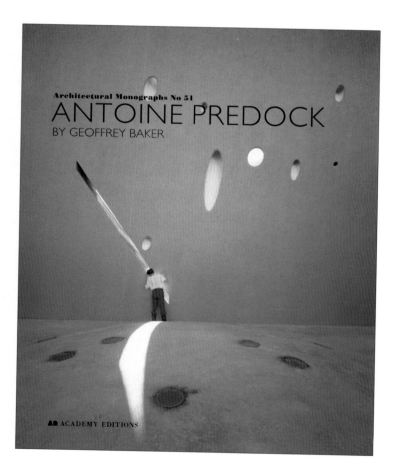

ANTOINE PREDOCK

Architectural Monographs No 49

Geoffrey Baker

Despite an international reputation, extensive educational and lecture tours across the globe, as well as a profusion of articles in journals, this is the first British publication devoted solely to the work of Antoine Predock, an American architect based in Albuquerque, New Mexico. Included is a large quantity of previously unpublished images and line drawings, affording a greater insight into the working methods of the architect. Among the many projects featured are the Turtle Creek House in Dallas, the Nelson Fine Arts Center, the National Archives of Denmark and the Arizona Science Center.

Geoffrey Baker teaches at the School of Architecture at Tulane University, New Orleans, and is the author of numerous books and articles on the work of architects such as James Stirling and Le Corbusier.

PB 0 471 97772 1, 305 x 252 mm, 128 pages, Illustrated throughout, mainly in colour, £21.95 $38.00 DM57.00: October 1997

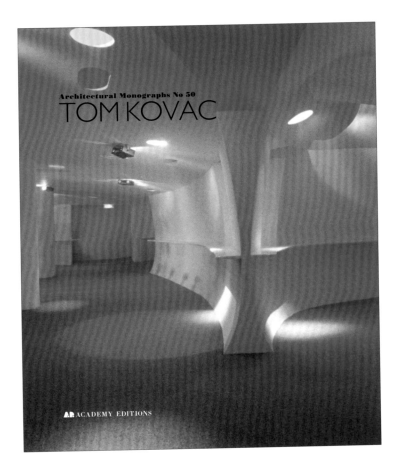

TOM KOVAC

Architectural Monographs No 50

Aaron Betsky, Leon van Schaik et al

Tom Kovac is an Australian architect who is rapidly gaining international fame with his fresh, dynamic work which denies a perception of architecture as a series of planes and right angles. His work does not evolve from a theoretical or rationalist standpoint, nor is it part of the tradition of urbanism, it is essentially concerned with pure form. His fluid spaces are emotionally charged and have recently begun to be published in journals worldwide. Projects in this first monograph on the architect's work include a variety of retail, commercial and residential buildings in Australia and the Pacific Rim, such as the Cherry Tree Hotel, the Gan House, Succhi and Atlas.

Aaron Betsky is an architectural critic based in San Francisco. Leon van Schaik is Dean of the Royal Melbourne Institute of Technology in Australia.

PB 0 471 97749 7, 305 x 252 mm, 128 pages. Illustrated throughout. £21.95 $38.00 DM57.00: October 1997

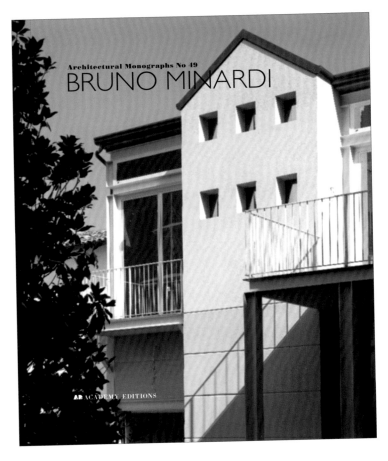

BRUNO MINARDI

Architectural Monographs No 51

Paulo Portoghesi

Although the designs and writings of Italian architect and professor Bruno Minardi have been published internationally, this is the first monograph on his work to appear in English. Often linked with Aldo Rossi, his tutor at Venice University, the strong theoretical thread which runs through Minardi's work is shown through his continued concern for the urban type and strong geometrical forms. This beautiful volume (designed with Minardi himself) presents the architect's recurring themes of attention to context and rapport with existing architecture and features projects throughout Europe, focusing on those in Italy. It also includes a selection of his watercolours and etchings.

Paulo Portoghesi is an architect based in Rome. He was editor of *Controspazio* and *Itaca* magazines.

PB 0 471 97854 X, 305 x 252 mm, 128 pages. Illustrated throughout, mainly in colour. £21.95 $38.00 DM57.00: October 1997

Books

Thirteen Ways: Theoretical Investigations in Architecture *by Robert Harbison, The MIT Press (Cambridge, MA), 1997, 205pp, 10b/w ills, HB £12.50*

The architectural profession claims a monopoly over architectural design for the purpose of economic and social self-protection. Although unregulated by the law, the architectural historian claims a similar monopoly within the field of history. Architects and architectural historians protect their territories by deriding incursions from outside as ignorant or mistaken, implying that there is a truthful and correct interpretation of a fixed body of knowledge. They monitor and patrol their domains to exclude critics from within and intruders from without, especially each other. Although the antagonism between architects and historians is a familiar one, Robert Harbison's fight is between historians and theorists. Of course, the ghost of the former antagonism remains in his argument. Although most architects are neither theorists nor historians, they are more likely to be the former than the latter, especially in the architectural world represented by magazines such as this.

Harbison obviously feels embattled. As he sides with history against the (perceived) onslaught of theory, the subtitle of his book, *Theoretical Investigations in Architecture*, is both ironic and confrontational. Harbison dislikes theory. He wants to defend history but not to write it, at least in the conventional sense of a factually 'verifiable' linear argument. Maybe he accepts that history is also an idea and objectivity a myth. Ironically for one who places himself on the side of history he has produced a book *against* history, more likely to anger historians than theorists. Many of his criticisms (of theory) are really manifestations of (his own) taste and sensibility, but then every text, including an historical one, is made by someone. Harbison condemns the *brutality* of Eisenman's geometry and the numbing consistency of Mies van der Rohe's IIT. Heartless is a term he uses often, but to whose *heart* does he refer? Taste and common sense are both a mask for ideology.

Thirteen Ways could only very loosely be described as a history. It could just about be called a theory. But really it is neither. Instead of historian or theorist, the term writer is a far more appropriate one to describe Harbison, whose enjoyment of language is clear, not always the case in texts written by historians or theorists. While Harbison denigrates contemporary literary theory, his own book is clearly informed by it. I am sure he must recognise, with irony, that the theory he criticises and the poem he praises share a number of themes and attitudes to writing. Derived from Wallace Stevens' poem *Thirteen Ways of Looking at a Blackbird*, Harbison's title is itself paradoxical. The text on the book jacket forewarns us that although Stevens' poem has thirteen elements, Harbison's book does not have thirteen chapters, merely ten, each with a simple title: sculpture, machines, the body, landscape, models, ideas, politics, the sacred, subjectivity, memory. The book is full of such conscious contradictions, one of its best characteristics. The reader is enticed to construct a new text from the fragments, finding or inventing the missing three elements.

The chapters are sandwiched between the book's most revealing elements, a very short preface and afterword in which the author speaks most directly to the reader. The linearity of thought and the primacy of vision are the dominant modes of intellectual operation within architectural discourse and production. Harbison refutes both assumptions. The book has a fractured narrative and few photographs. However, paradoxically, form, to which vision is coupled, is the real subject of this book. Joseph Rykwert is correct to categorise Harbison's text as collage, as it affirms a crucial distinction between collage and montage. While the former is primarily an aesthetic strategy, the latter, through its greater emphasis on context, is both political and critical. Harbison's use of juxtaposition is often witty but opaque, for example that of Mae West and Jesus Christ. Indeed the pleasure of this text appears in the fragments, which are often subtle and stimulating. Stevens' poem, from which Harbison derives his 'shattered or oblique structure', contains one element that Harbison's text lacks, a subject as simple and direct as the blackbird. Stevens' poem says far less about the blackbird than any one of Harbison's chapters does about its subject. But the poem works because we all have a clear idea of what a blackbird is. If the (notional) subject of the poem is the blackbird, architecture fulfils a similar role in Harbison's book, but is too contentious and slippery to bind the narrative together.

Harbison's book is defined by its author's criticism of theory. At a conference I attended a few years ago, Harbison, in witty and self-deprecating terms, bemoaned the 'triumph' of theory over history, outlining the criticisms of theory repeated in his latest book. As is so often the case, the critic fashions the subject of (his) criticism into a repository of negativity qualities. For Harbison, theory is rigid, cruel and joyless. However, at the same conference, Brian Hatton responded to Harbison with a subtle question: if he could write a book on eccentric spaces, why could he not write one on eccentric theories?

Jonathan Hill

Reviews
Books

Le Corbusier – The Creative Search: The formative years of Charles-Edouard Jeanneret *by Geoffrey H Baker, E&F Spon (London) 1996, 320pp, colour and b/w ills, HB*

Baker's previously published study, *Le Corbusier: An Analysis of Form*, deals primarily with design issues in relation to Le Corbusier's built work. This recent volume is to some extent complementary and was conceived around the same time. However, here the sketches form the backbone of the study; principally those produced by Le Corbusier (the pseudonym adopted by Jeanneret in 1920) at the Art School in La Chaux-de-Fonds (1901-1905) and on his study trips in Italy (1907) and the East (1911).

In his quest to uncover more about the creative development of this much publicised figure, Baker assembles an eclectic range of drawings and watercolours from the early period, many of which are reproduced here in colour. Typically, the subject matter includes mountain ranges, rock formations, trees, flowers, insects, clouds, frescos, sculpture, medieval buildings, architectural details, decorative motifs. These drawings were research vehicles which enabled Le Corbusier to determine the underlying forces and structure of nature. Some are more impressionistic and atmospheric in nature, such as the earlier landscapes which convey varying natural conditions; others are more intricately detailed and depict elements which he extracted, analysed and then transformed.

For one who lacked an academic education as such, the training at La Chaux-de-Fonds must have been crucial to the young Jeanneret. He would have been an impressionable fourteen-year-old when he enrolled in the school as an apprentice engraver; transferring to the architecture course three years later. Baker provides useful insights into this early environment, examining in depth the influence of his teacher L'Eplattenier and the publications to which Le Corbusier had access. Though Le Corbusier was later to find fault with L'Eplattenier, he was an important medium in imparting the lessons of Ruskin, Owen Jones and Grasset whose writings instilled in him a lifelong belief in the value and relationship of nature to the design process (initially consummated in the Villa Fallet, designed with Rene Chapallaz).

The extent to which Le Corbusier was influenced by publications is debated throughout the book. Known to be in his possession earlier on were *l'Art de demain* by Henry Provensal and Edouard Schuré's *Les grands inities*. In the former, the artist is seen as a link in uniting man with the 'absolute' (revealed through divine laws described as unity, number and harmony); it was Provensal's belief that the new art would evolve through the medium of architecture and be of an abstract nature. Baker draws on the research of Paul Turner (author of *The Education of Le Corbusier*) who noted a correlation between Le Corbusier's later definition that 'architecture is the masterly correct and magnificent arrangement of masses brought together in light' and Provensal's definition: 'The oppositions of shade and light, volume and void, expressed critically in three dimensions, constitutes one of the most beautiful plastic dramas in the world'.

In the first five chapters Baker analyses in detail the glut of sketches, watercolours and annotations Le Corbusier produced in Italy, Austria, Paris, Germany and the East. He examines Le Corbusier's technique and approach, explaining how he had already decided the nature of what a subject held for him before he put pen to paper; thus watercolour is used for the interior of the cathedral, Siena (depicted on the cover) in order to recapture the effect of light on coloured marble surfaces; while more intricately detailed sketches exploit the three-dimensional aspects of a subject.

Concurrently, insights are given into his philosophical development, such as the impact of Nietzsche's *Thus Spake Zarathustra* and Renan's *Life of Jesus*. At this time he was working for Perret and while extolling the virtues of Romanesque architecture in a letter to L'Eplattenier of 1908, Le Corbusier communicated, somewhat bitterly, his ignorance about modern architecture. He was exposed to an entirely new and stimulating approach to building and materials under Auguste Perret (whose office building, Baker observes, included four of Le Corbusier's five points: pilotis, free plan, free facade, roof garden; with the exception of ribbon windows).

Le Corbusier's belief in the necessity for a fresh approach and the role of art as essential to man's progress was consolidated by his journey to the East. Much of what he absorbed (for example, the ability of architecture to exploit topography) was realised on his return to La Chaux-de-Fonds in 1911, to which Baker devotes a chapter. With reference to the Villa Jeanneret-Perret, he describes how in terms of spatial progression and cubic volume, the design reflected his overriding interest in the Acropolis, forecasting the *promenade architecturale*. The rational, economic and standardised approach inherent in the Dom-ino proposals also reflected Le Corbusier's appreciation of vernacular dwelling forms and represented a departure from the more decorative vernacular of the earlier projects, initiating the more cool and abstract classicism of the Villa Schwob.

Baker's analysis of Le Corbusier's creative development is thorough and well informed. He communicates the underlying motivation of the drawings from this era with great clarity and is keen to impress upon the reader their lasting influence on Le Corbusier's work, believing that an understanding of his architecture is incomplete without knowledge of these drawings. Throughout the book he cites examples in which they were constantly referred to for inspiration at every stage in Le Corbusier's career.

The scope of the book is therefore extensive and allows a complete picture of Le Corbusier's emerging philosophy and creative output to develop; encompassing *Vers une architecture* and *Urbanisme*, Purism, and the liberating effect of painting on Le Corbusier's architectural language. Le Corbusier is also seen in relation to architects such as Aalto, Meier, Venturi, and Norberg-Schulz. A useful feature of the book is the way the information has been organised with concise descriptions of illustrations separated from the main text for further analysis; as a result, the flow of text remains uninterrupted. Although this study will be shelved amidst a stack of publications devoted to every aspect of Le Corbusier's work, it is a valuable addition.

Iona Spens

Reviews
Books

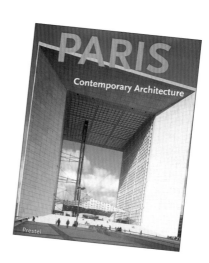

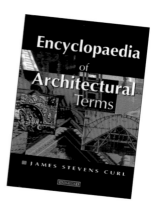

Architectural History and the Studio, *edited by Adam Hardy and Necdet Teymur, ?uestion Press (London), 1996, 212pp, 38 b/w ills, PB £11.95*
Based on the premise that the architecture of today is crucially dependent on its interpretation of the past, this collection of essays addresses the relationship between architectural design and the teaching of architectural history. Contributors include David Dunster, Robert Harbison and Katerina Ruedi.

The Struggle for Utopia: Rodchenko, Lissitzky, Moholy-Nagy 1917-1946, *by Victor Margolin (2nd edition), the University of Chicago Press (Chicago), 1997, 274pp, 107 b/w ills, HB $39.95*
The artist-designers Alexander Rodchenko, El Lissitzky and László Moholy-Nagy were central figures in the artistic-social avant-garde movement which emerged between the Wars. Margolin analyses their works in the context of the political and social upheavals of the era, documenting their contributions to utopian architecture, Constructivist ideology, industrial design, photography, visual communication and design education.

Intelligent Spaces: Architecture for the Information Age, *by Otto Riewoldt, Laurence King Publishing (London), 1997, 240pp, 354 mostly col ills, HB £45.00*
Is architecture keeping pace with the electronic revolution of the 1990s? This survey of 50 highly-serviced building projects in Europe, the USA and the Far East addresses the question of how the forms and functions of architecture have evolved to meet changing technology. The 50 case studies fall into one of five categories; multimedia industries; banks and financial institutions; multi-functional complexes; 'infotainment' centres and cultural and educational institutions.

Paris: Contemporary Architecture, *by Andrea Gleiniger, Gerhard Matzig and Sebastian Redecke, Prestel (Munich and New York), 1997, 160pp, 261 col and b/w ills, HB £35.00*
A critical analysis of architecture constructed in Paris during the past decade. Projects selected range from the internationally-acclaimed (Parc de la Villette, Bibliothèque François Mitterrand) through major context-related planning schemes (the Bercy and André Citroën parks) to lesser-known government housing schemes and housing projects.

Seven Partly Underground Rooms and Buildings for Water, Ice and Midgets, *by Mary-Ann Ray, Pamphlet Architecture No 20 , Princeton Architectural Press (New York), 1997, 78pp, b/w ills, PB £8.95*
Documentation of Mary-Ann Ray's analytical investigations into the typology of seven Italian spaces, with a short introduction by Steven Holl.

A Passage Through Silence and Light: Daniel Libeskind's Jewish Museum Extension to the Berlin Museum, *photographs by Hélène Binet, Black Dog Publishing Ltd (London), 1997*
A series of photographs taken during the construction of Libeskind's Jewish Museum, which is intended to encapsulate transient phases in the building's life.

Encyclopaedia of Architectural Terms *by James Stevens Curl, Donhead (Dorset), 1997, 364pp, b/w ills, PB £19.95*
The first paperback edition of this reference work which provides a comprehensive guide to architectural and building terminology – 3,500 entries define styles, the components of buildings, materials, the parts of the Classical Orders, and architectural details.

NEW SCIENCE = NEW ARCHITECTURE?

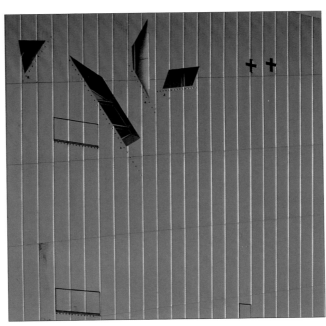

DANIEL LIBESKIND, THE BERLIN MUSEUM WITH THE JEWISH MUSEUM, BERLIN

Architectural Design

NEW SCIENCE = NEW ARCHITECTURE?

OPPOSITE: EISENMAN ARCHITECTS, ARONOFF CENTER FOR DESIGN AND ART, UNIVERSITY OF CINCINNATI, OHIO;
ABOVE: FRANK O GEHRY, THE GUGGENHEIM MUSEUM, BILBAO, SPAIN

ACADEMY EDITIONS · LONDON

Acknowledgements

We would like to express our gratitude to Charles Jencks for guest-editing this issue of *Architectural Design* and all the contributors to the New Science = New Architecture? Academy Forum which was held at the Royal Academy of Arts, London on 5 November 1996, in particular, MaryAnne Stevens and Sir Philip Dowson. We are grateful to the following for contributing to this issue: Mae-Wan Ho and Peter Saunders, Peter Eisenman, Frank O Gehry, Daniel Libeskind, Cecil Balmond, Michael Batty and Paul Longley, Ben van Berkel and Caroline Bos, Farshid Moussavi and Alejandro Zaero-Polo, and Ashton Raggatt McDougall. We would also like to thank Jeff Goldberg, the photographer at Esto, for his permission to reproduce photographs of The Aronoff Center for Design and Art, University of Cincinnati; Carlos Iturriaga, the Project Manager of the Guggenheim Museum, Bilbao, for providing images of the museum; and The Natural History Museum, London for featuring specimens from its collection.

Photographic Credits: all material is courtesy of the authors and architects unless otherwise stated. Attempts have been made to locate the sources of all photographs to obtain full reproduction rights, but in the very few cases where this process has failed to find the copyright holder, our apologies are offered. Ove Arup *p91 centre and below*; The Australian National Museum, Melbourne *p8 above left*; Cecil Balmond *inside covers, pp89 right, 90, 91 above, 92-3, 94 above centre and left, 95*; Bitter Bredt Fotografie *pp59-62*; Dick Frank *p12*; Jeff Goldberg/Esto *pp2, 10, 11, 14, 19*; John Gollings *p26 below*; The Guggenheim Museum, Bilbao/Aitor Ortiz *front cover, pp3, 30-34, 35 above and below, 38-9 above*; Ariel Huber *pp64 below, 66*; Katsuhisa Kida *p9 above right*; Kenji Kobayashi *p9 above left*; Rem Koolhaas *pp88, 89 centre and left*; Hans-Jurgen Commerell *p87*; Peter Kulka *p94 above left and below*; Edward Woodman *p64 above*

Front Cover: The Guggenheim Museum, Bilbao, Spain, 1993-97, Frank O Gehry, *photo: Aitor Ortiz*
Inside covers: Victoria & Albert Museum fractal, *Cecil Balmond*

EDITOR: Maggie Toy
PRODUCTION EDITOR: Ellie Duffy
ART EDITOR: Alex Young

First published in Great Britain in 1997 by *Architectural Design*, an imprint of
ACADEMY GROUP LTD, 42 LEINSTER GARDENS, LONDON W2 3AN

A division of John Wiley & Sons
Baffins Lane, Chichester, West Sussex PO19 IUD

ISBN: 0-471-97739-X

Architectural Design Profile 129 is published as part of
Architectural Design Vol 67 9-10 /1997
Architectural Design Magazine is published six times a year and is available by subscription

Distributed to the trade in the United States of America by
NATIONAL BOOK NETWORK INC, 4720 BOSTON WAY, LANHAM, MARYLAND, 20706

Printed and bound in Italy

Contents

ARCHITECTURAL DESIGN PROFILE No 129
NEW SCIENCE = NEW ARCHITECTURE?
Guest-Edited by Charles Jencks

DANIEL LIBESKIND, MODEL OF THE VICTORIA & ALBERT MUSEUM BOILERHOUSE EXTENSION

Charles Jencks Nonlinear Architecture: New Science = New Architecture? *6*

Complexity Definition and Nature's Complexity *8*

Eisenman Architects Aronoff Center for Design and Art, University of Cincinnati, Ohio *10*

Charles Jencks Landform Architecture: Emergent in the Nineties *14*

Frank O Gehry The Guggenheim Museum, Bilbao *32*

Charles Jencks The Surface of Complexity: The Work of Frank O Gehry *36*

Ashton Raggatt McDougall Storey Hall, Melbourne *40*

Mae-Wan Ho The New Age of the Organism *44*

Peter T Saunders Nonlinearity: What it is and Why it Matters *52*

Daniel Libeskind Between the Lines *58*

The Victoria & Albert Museum Boilerhouse Extension, London *64*

Foreign Office Architects Yokohama International Port Terminal, Yokohama *68*

Michael Batty and Paul Longley The Fractal City *74*

Van Berkel & Bos Erasmus Bridge, Rotterdam *84*

Cecil Balmond New Structure and the Informal *88*

NONLINEAR ARCHITECTURE

NEW SCIENCE = NEW ARCHITECTURE?

Charles Jencks

Over the last 100 years many architects have proclaimed a new architecture based on emergent conditions of life. Ironically, under the Modernists, these proclamations became traditional as they resulted in yet one more version of the quite familiar: it was often not new, nor really architecture but rather building illustrating a novel idea. Hence the exasperation of Mies: 'one cannot have a new architecture every Monday morning'; hence the scepticism of the Old Modernists as they confronted the epoch of fashion, and a fast change that went nowhere.

However, another argument can be made – the premise of this issue of *AD* – which highlights a shift in philosophy and worldview. According to this, when there is a change in the basic framework of thought then there has to be a shift in architecture because this, like other forms of cultural expression, is embedded in the reigning mental paradigms. The question then becomes partly sociological: whether we really do have a new science, one different from the old modern linear sciences which grew from the Newtonian paradigm. Much has been claimed for the new sciences of complexity. These, the Santa Fe Institute predicts, will complement the reductivist sciences of the last 300 years. But, have the post-modern sciences of nonlinear dynamics sublimated the old ones? Are fractals and self-organising systems more general than Euclidean geometry and mechanistic systems? Are they more attuned to nature than linear mechanics? How far have scientists accepted complexity theories as primary explanations?

As Mae-Wan Ho and Peter Saunders suggest later, the mechanical, linear paradigm of science has been superseded: this does not mean that the scientific community, or a majority of scientists, now agree on the nonlinear paradigm; in fact, they may not even agree on positive formulations. The mechanistic world view may have ended (nails in its coffin from quantum physics to chaos science over 80 years have seen to that) but there is no single heir such as organicism, complexity science, nonlinear dynamics, the new genetics, etc. They may be compatible but they command no single voice and theory. Yet, Mae-Wan Ho and Peter Saunders, in their explanations of the new science, and vigorous speculation, show very clearly what is at stake; a universe where, in Mae-Wan's words, there can be *reverse* information, back from RNA to DNA, where 'genes can jump horizontally', where 'intercommunication is instantaneous or nonlocal'. These, and many more wild facts which the new sciences are revealing, throw the mechanistic paradigm into doubt and lead us to assume that the universe is a lot more creative, free, self-organising and open than Newton, Darwin and others supposed.

If we assume that there is a new science, and a *partial* consensus about its worth, the next question becomes: what are the recent exemplars of this new paradigm? Here, the answer includes the buildings presented in this issue, above all three of the seminal buildings of the 90s: Frank Gehry's Guggenheim Museum in Bilbao, Peter Eisenman's Aronoff Center in Cincinnati and Daniel Libeskind's Jewish Extension to the Berlin Museum. All three are Nonlinear buildings and were partly generated by nonlinear methods including computer design and layout. Each one raises critical questions about the role of metaphor in architecture: that is, choosing and modifying a language of continuous variation and discovering new meanings inherent in its use. New Science = new language = new metaphors. Architecture not only reflects a different paradigm of thought but itself becomes a discipline of unfolding knowledge. The engineering inventions of Cecil Balmond, the aperiodic and fractal tiling of ARM, and other innovations extend architectural thought. As I will argue, it also may take responsibility for metaphorical invention.

Another issue is whether the paradigm is consciously pursued or not: are we seeing merely a parallel between science and architecture or something deeper? Is it only a question of using computers and designing curved buildings – a fashion – or a change in the mental landscape? Philip Johnson's recent conversion to the paradigm, evident in his Monsta House, suggests it is both. To be specific: how much do architects understand of fractals, emergence theory, folding, nonlinearity and self-organising systems? How much is this a formalist trend? Can they furnish a new iconography, a new style and set of meanings? Can one design a whole city fabric in their image?

The most profound question is: Why does it matter? Is the new Nonlinear Architecture somehow superior, closer to nature and our understanding of the cosmos, than Old Modernism? Is it more sensuous, functional, liveable? Is it closer to aesthetic codes which are built into perception? Has it supplanted the traditions from which it has grown – Post-Modern and Deconstructivist architecture? The answer to these questions, which implicitly justify a change, might be 'yes', but it is too early to tell. There are other supporting arguments of a cultural and spiritual nature: architecture, to be true to the spirit of contemporary life and the life of forms in art, must explore new languages. Many will find this justification enough. A new urban language is evident in ARM's Storey Hall, one which could provide an order as understandable as the classical and modern, yet more variable and surprising.

Further innovations, or mutations in this emergent tradition, include the land-form building. The landscape as building has emerged as a new complex type and now there are quite a few built examples to judge: those by Eisenman, Miralles, Koolhaas, Gehry, Ben van Berkel and those about to be constructed by Foreign Office Architects and Morphosis. Partly motivated by maximum return on real-estate, a cynical realism, they are also intended to return architecture to a greater landscape tradition. There are several more motives at work in this runaway paradigm – its plural goals and styles are irreducible – so Nonlinear Architecture will prosper as a major movement into the millennium, fed by the new sciences of complexity. My particular hopes for its direction are outlined on page 15, but wherever it goes this new approach will challenge both the Newtonian and traditional architecture that have gone before.

Frank O Gehry, The Guggenheim Museum, Bilbao, Spain, 1993-97

COMPLEXITY DEFINITION AND NATURE'S COMPLEXITY

Charles Jencks

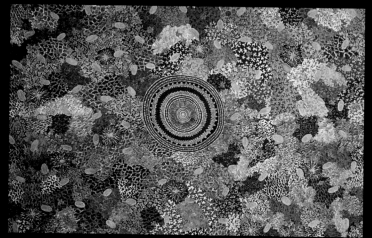

M Tjampitjinpa, Bush Banana Dreaming, *1986.*

In the last few years there have been over 30 definitions of Complexity but none has achieved canonic status, so here is a compound definition:

Complexity is the theory of how emergent organisation may be achieved by interacting components pushed far from equilibrium (by increasing energy, matter or information) to the threshold between order and chaos. This important border or threshold is where the system often jumps, bifurcates or creatively interacts in a new nonlinear, unpredictable way (the Eureka moment) and where the new organisation may be sustained through feedback and the continuous input of energy.

In this process quality emerges spontaneously as self-organisation, meaning, value, openness, fractal patterns, attractor formations and (often) increasing complexity (a greater degree of freedom).

The direction of the universe? Or its narrative?

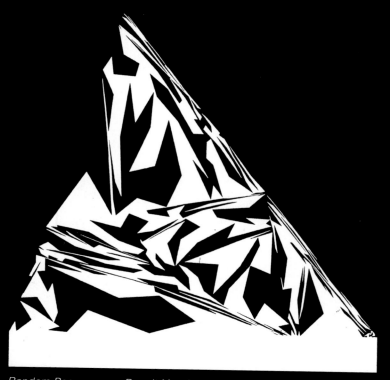

Random Peano curve, Benoit Mandelbrot. The following generator, acting on the initiatior (0,1) yields a way of sweeping a triangle: N=4, R=1/2, D=2.

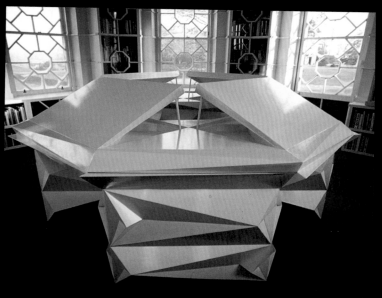

Charles Jencks, Fractal Table, Scotland, 1995.

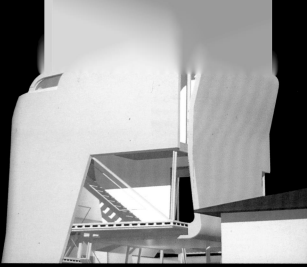

Neil Denari, Beverly Hills House, 1996 – Nonlinear Architecture made from a single bent surface, cut and spliced in parts for light and function.

Ushida Findlay Partnership, Truss Wall House, Tokyo, 1993.

Interior of Truss Wall House.

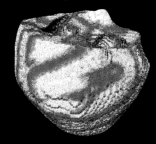
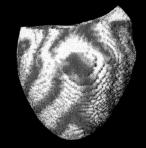
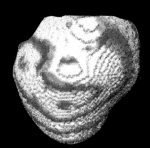
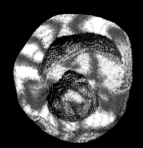

Dr Arun Holden, computer model of a virtual heart, Leeds University, 1995, visualised from four sides in its holistic behaviour; the electrical waves go from self-similar order (alive) to quivering fibrillation.

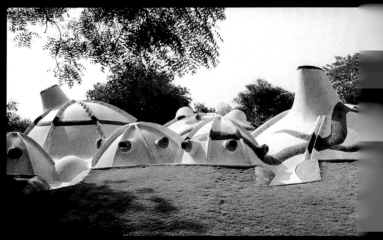

Balkrishna Doshi, Hussain-Doshi Gufa, Ahmedabad, India, 1995, underground interior of domes showing movement and torsion.

Hussain-Dosi Gufa, exterior of ribbed domes inspired by traditional and modern cosmology, made from reinforced concrete and wire mesh.

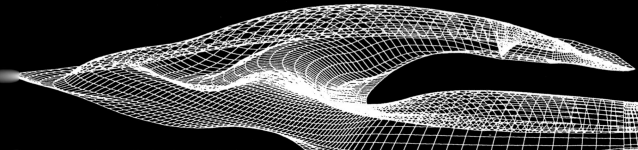

Shoei Yoh Architects, Uchino Community Centre, 1995, computer-generated image of roof framework.

EISENMAN ARCHITECTS
ARONOFF CENTER FOR DESIGN AND ART
University of Cincinnati, Ohio

The new building for the University of Cincinnati was completed in autumn 1996. The initial phase of work at the university involved developing a brief for the College of Design, Architecture, Art and Planning which would reorganise the existing 145,000 square feet of the building and provide an additional 128,000 square feet of exhibition, library, theatre, studio and office space. The architects were also requested to improve the quality, quantity and accessibility of the college facilities.

The scheme which developed from brief unified the four schools within the college, thereby encouraging interdisciplinary exchange and alleviating the extreme overcrowding presently experienced by administrators, faculty and students. The initial challenge was that the context – the physical site, the existing building, and the spirit of the college – should determine the form of the building. Its vocabulary derives from the curves of the land forms and the chevron forms of the existing structure; the dynamic relationship between these two forms organises the space between them.

The project evolved as a collaborative effort with the students, faculty, administrators and friends of the college. Thus the building was conceived not as an architectural monument but as the product of an evolutionary process of work, created by everyone.

The objective of the scheme is to challenge and transform the way people are educated: to discourage the design of the superficial and the inconsequential. Design disciplines must assume a far more important role in this media-dominated information age. The Center is designed to express these sentiments about society and the role of design.

In 1991 the project won the Architectural Design Award from *Progressive Architecture* and was exhibited at the Fifth International Exhibition of Architecture of the Venice Biennale.

Jeff Goldberg/Esto

Jeff Goldberg/Esto

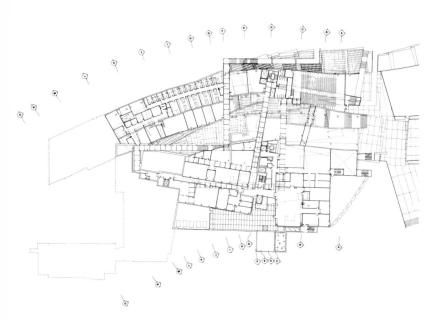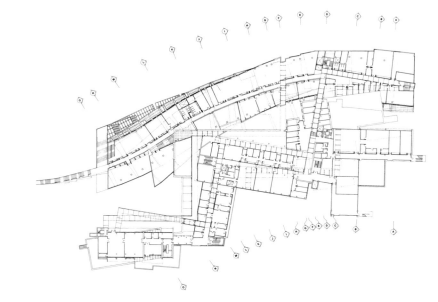

ABOVE L TO R: Plans – 400 level, 600 level, 700 level;
BELOW: Aerial view of site model

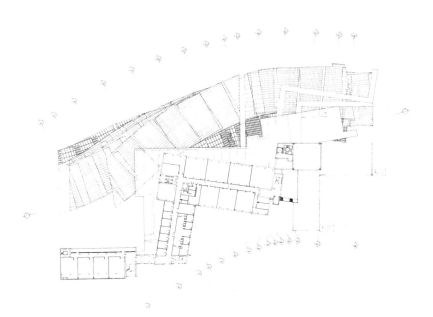

13

LANDFORM ARCHITECTURE
EMERGENT IN THE NINETIES

Charles Jencks

The complexity paradigm in architecture, based loosely around the sciences of complexity, has reached maturity. Two traditions have developed in parallel: one in architecture, another in science. These overlap fortuitously and, in the case of architecture, consciously. Some of the architects I will discuss here consciously adopt the underlying ideas of nonlinear science and its many suggestive methods of production and design.

Three major buildings of the early 1990s are finished or nearly so – Peter Eisenman's Aronoff Center, Daniel Libeskind's Jewish Museum and Frank Gehry's Bilbao Museum – and work by lesser known architects such as Enric Miralles, Zvi Hecker, the groups ARM and Ushida Findlay has widened this growing tradition. While it does not dominate professional practice – thankfully no approach does – it is moving into a central position without losing vigour. This sustained, broadening creativity is one of its most promising aspects. Surprisingly, even quite a few High-Tech architects are flirting with the paradigm and one of the best of them, Nicholas Grimshaw, has complex structures nearing completion. Complexity Building, Cosmogenic Design, Nonlinear Architecture, call it what you will, is extending and deepening its roots and now has many practitioners.[1]

The work I will discuss here is part of this emergent tradition, the part concerned with an issue close to urban design and Earth Art: that is, how can one handle a large volume of city building without becoming too monumental, cliched or oppressive in scale. One of the answers is the landform building: architecture as articulated landscape. There are opposite forces creating the landform structure, such as real estate pressure to cram as much activity into the tightest space possible (something that leads to the shed space) and the idea that environmental forces – wind, gravity, the flow of traffic – and the landscape as a site of tectonic activity, can inspire new thinking. Between cynicism and inspiration landform architecture is emerging as one of the most potent ideas today. Rather than merely illustrate the new paradigm with examples, I will discuss several buildings in depth, analyzing their quality as architecture, since ultimately it is this quality that matters.

From matter to *mutter*

Peter Eisenman's addition to Cincinnati University is one of the first completed essays in the genre. It stacks up different activities and spaces on to a pre-existing building, just as one geological formation pushes sediment and rock on to another. The result is part collision – the earthquake of forms that everyone comments on – and part intermeshing of tectonic plates. A new kind of grammar results from these waves of compression: a staccato, clunky, somewhat awkward language which, nevertheless, has its own peculiar grace. Why is this? After having visited the building twice I have come to the conclusion that it is because the volumes are mid-scale, often about the size of a person and always subtly changing, thus

constantly attracting our interest. They become a new form of ornament that roots the body in what would otherwise be a labyrinth of confusion.

These mid-scale forms weave in an out of each other like tartan, or shake and tilt against each other like shards after an avalanche. The logic behind these stuttering cubes – and Eisenman, like Palladio, invites the user to become involved in the high game of architecture – is a colour code marking the design process. Light blues, flesh pinks and greens relate what chunk belongs to what design idea and why it is shifted or tilted or shimmering. The overall result is a new system which, in an unlikely comparison, reminds me of the Rococo, or the pastel delicacies of Robert Adam. Rococo also shimmers in fractured planes of light and Adamesque architecture has a similar colour-tone but the prettiness and conventionality of both could not have been further from Eisenman's intention.

He seeks to provoke and shock, to decentre perspective, deprivilege any one point of view, cross boundaries, blur categories (especially the boundary between the old stepped building and his new segmental attachment). 'There is no preferred place for the viewer to understand', Eisenman says, invoking the contradictory perspectival space of Piranesi.[2] To achieve these multiple-readings he has adopted several different methods which, characteristically, are diagrammed clearly, so that aficionados can follow the moves. Chevrons are tilted back and forth off the existing building; they set up one system against which a segmental line – mostly of studio space – is played. This line is 'torqued', 'overlapped', and 'stepped' both as a solid and void. Other moves are made, which I find impossible to understand (could 'phase shift' really be a 'tilt'?). But the result is a relatively new way of generating a sensual architecture.

Inevitably, such a complexity of different formal strategies could only be worked out on a computer and built by using laser technology and a special coordinate system of construction points. Since a team of engineers and contractors had to be trained to create this new architecture, it is a pity no film was made during production; so, if it is ever repeated in the future, the system will have to be reinvented. One of the most convincing parts of the interior is near the main entrance from the garage side. One comes through a hybrid grid – of window/door/wall – into a symphony of staggered, staccato forms. Overhead, skylights and fluorescent tubes cut up chunks of space; below one's feet, cheap vinyl tile marks the interweaving systems, while the pastel cubes to either side dovetail and layer through each other. The 2,000 students who stream through to the art and architectural lessons will be kept tense and alert by these cut-up fragments. At the same time the forms make no semantic demand, have no figural message; they are completely abstract.

Eisenman Architects (with Lorenz and Williams), Aronoff Center for Design and Art, University of Cincinnati, 1989-96, view of atrium

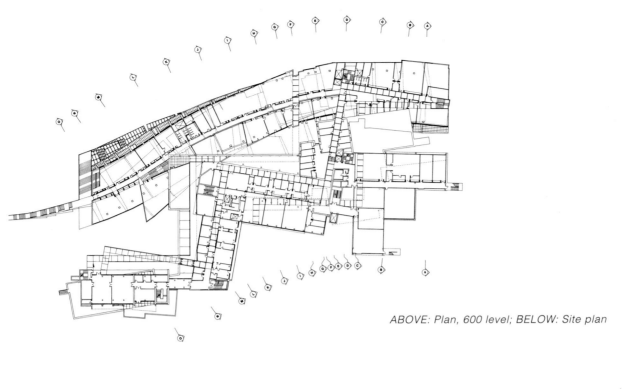

ABOVE: Plan, 600 level; BELOW: Site plan

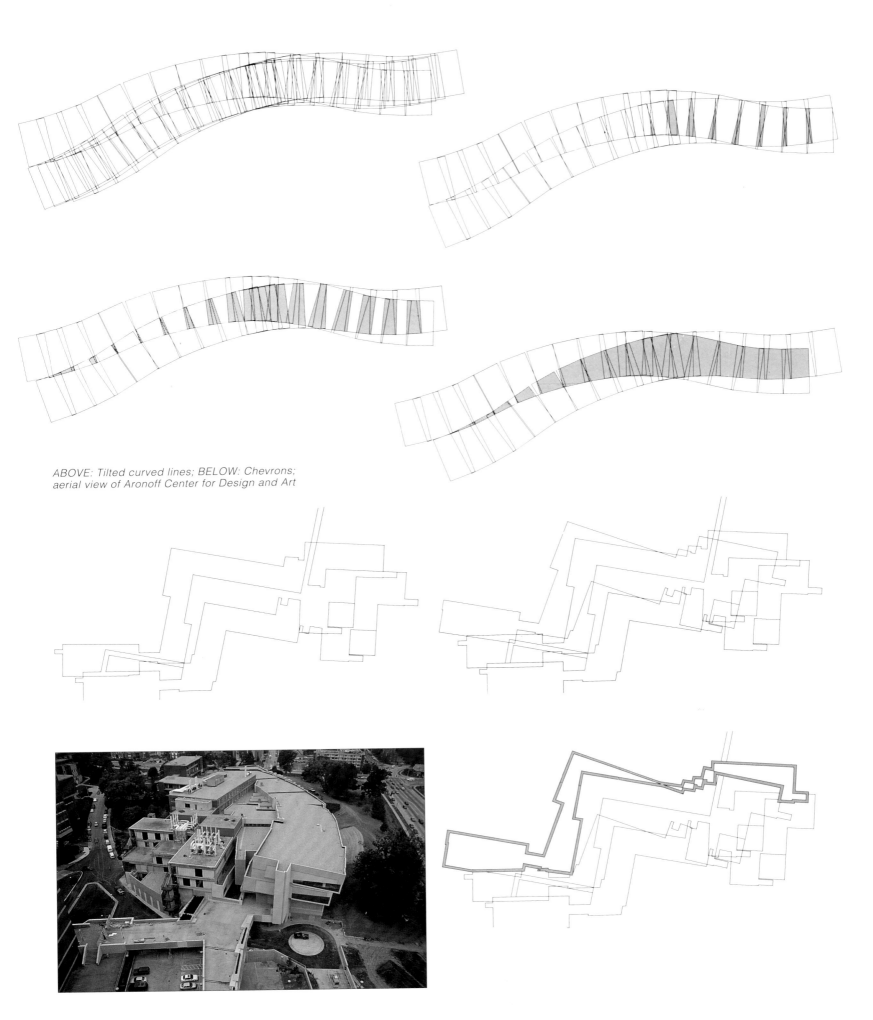

ABOVE: Tilted curved lines; BELOW: Chevrons;
aerial view of Aronoff Center for Design and Art

Aronoff Center for Design and Art, drawing of atrium

The lack of representational form (aside from the overall 'earthquake') can be considered a virtue for a modest, infill building, but there is one obvious problem with the whole scheme. Given its high degree of compression, its ceilings and walls pressing in everywhere, and given its very deep plan – a typical fact of life in the landform tradition – it cries out for release, for greenery, light from above, a view to the outside from the central atrium. This space, however, in spite of its inwardness, is another one of the small triumphs of the building. Atrium, plaza, square, piazza – the Spanish Steps? None of the prototypes of the public realm are invoked, but they are all implied by

the way the broad stairway mounts in gentle steps to one side of the triangular 'piazza' below (with its restaurant). This is a convivial social space mixing several uses, a public realm which only lacks nature and a symbolic focus.

On a positive level, Eisenman has created a new fabric which is always changing subtly, one in which the architectural drama consists in traces of the design methods pushing through each other. Basically, a set of seesawing, blue chevrons marks the old grid while the pink and green segments mark the new formal methods; a tilt to one side, an earthquake to another and the trapezoidal crush of windows and floors between. It is a new

Aronoff Center for Design and Art, promenade architecturale, *atrium looking west*

visual language of staccato landforms and straight tangents. As a geological metaphor, it is more mica than flowing lava, more awkward chunky crystals than the flowing landforms which characterise most building in the genre. Whereas Greg Lynn and Shoei Yoh propose more supple, continuous forms, a single roof that slides over different areas and only inflects a bit to accommodate a function, Eisenman's grammar is more charged. As Sanford Kwinter has argued, structures that interest late 20th-century scientists are often concerned with 'matter in the throes of creation'; that is, matter pushed far from equilibrium so that it self-organises.[3] This kind of matter is not inert and dead. The noble scientist Ilya Prigogine, who has done more to interpret the issues at stake than others, speaks in metaphorical terms about the way that blind matter – pushed far from equilibrium – can suddenly see. Per Bak's 'self-organising criticality', the theory of how sandpiles self-organise when they reach a critical state, is one example. Each piece of sand, when the pile reaches the critical angle, is in touch with every other one, can 'see every other one', and this sudden holistic organisation brings the system to life; or, rather, to lifelike dynamic behaviour. The same is true of tectonic plates pushed to critical compression, or any material system pushed to the threshold between order and chaos.

Eisenman Architects, Staten Island Institute of Arts and Sciences,
St George Ferry Terminal, New York, computer rendering

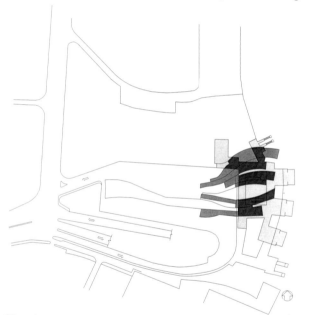

Site plan: arrow points north; water to the right of the ferry terminal

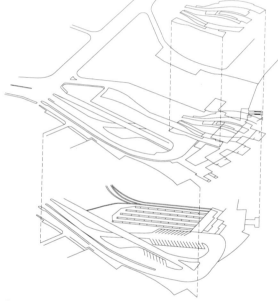

Axonometric overlays of various transportation methods

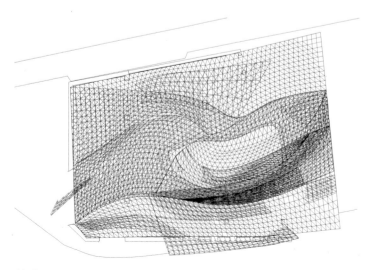

Horizontal section study, cut two-thirds of the way up on the building diagram

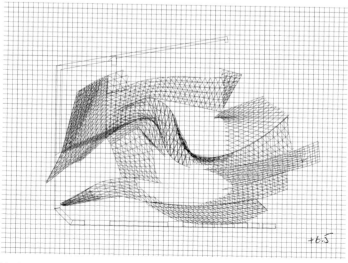

Horizontal section study, cut a third of the way up

Staten Island Institute of Arts and Sciences, computer rendering

Since all matter in this state transforms itself and becomes closer to the living organism I will christen it *mutter*, after the German for mother. Mother earth is an old metaphor of regeneration, but what I am implying is the potential for all dead matter to act, at the threshold of chaos, in a spontaneous, interactive way – as if it were free; as if it had a mind of its own, like a mother.

In a recent scheme for a museum and ferry terminal on Staten Island in New York, Eisenman has pushed the deep landform building in a more crystalline direction. White spirals of translucent glass and steel ratchet their way over a dense traffic intersection of boats, pedestrians, and buses. The flow of traffic becomes one generator of the forms, while wind and water also play a role.

Diagrams of laminar flow used to test aeroplanes and boats create a swirling grammar and Eisenman is also inspired by the fractal shapes of the Stealth Fighter. But, as rendered on the computer, this grammar is again chunky and staccato. It rises and curves in tangents, like an ice-flow bent around a rock.

Perhaps this metaphor reveals something about the design since the old terminal for the ferry – the rock – makes the new museum and circulation space, above it, twist and tilt. Here we are closer to Greg Lynn's ideal of a continuous structure deformed by circumstance, a flow-diagram punctuated by events. The shed-space and the super-skin, the real-estate realism and the cosmic gesture. Is it a Stealth Fighter, UFO, ice-flow, spiral of crystals, or layered laminar diagrams – or, simply, dense packing? In Britain, developers call repetitive close-packing 'rent-slab capitalism' and it has, deservedly, given Modern architecture a bad name.

How does this horrible truth impinge on the landform tradition? At Cincinnati, Eisenman really has subtracted the deep plan of its pathos and meanness. The reality is cheap, the materials minimal and ordinary – fluorescent tubes and linoleum – but these necessities have been transformed into an exciting symphony of very rich complexity. In effect, Eisenman has turned dumb matter into syncopated *mutter*. The shift in the sign works; it looks like it will again on Staten Island.

F-117A Stealth Fighter

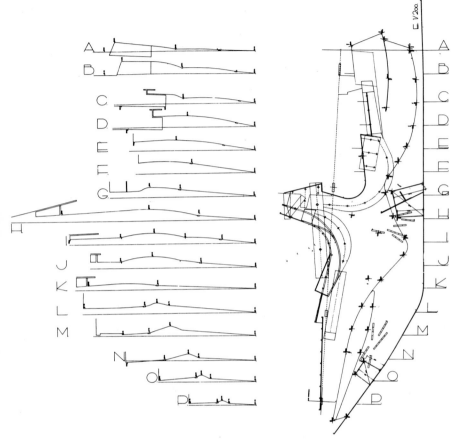

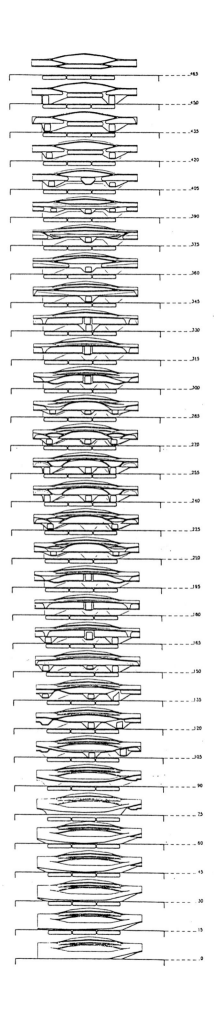

ABOVE: Enric Miralles, Eurhythmics Centre, Alicante, Spain, 1993-94, earth movements under entry ramps. The rise and spread of wave-forms from A to G and H to P can be felt through this 'cinematic sectioning'; BELOW: The rise and fall of the structure in jagged tangents 'borrows the mountainscape'

RIGHT: FOA, Yokohama International Port Terminal (competition winner, 1995), 'Cinematic sectioning' shows a folded plate in steel – a self-stiffening structure

The cinematic section

Enric Miralles, the Barcelona architect, has developed various notation systems for dealing with the landform building. He depicts the sprawling context of his buildings with a Hockneyesque method of photo-collage; that is, he splices together a continuous image of changing perspectives that wanders about in a higgledy-piggledy manner but still keeps a fractal identity, a self-similar quality. Secondly, he has devised what could be called 'cinematic sectioning': the analysis of a large land-mass by making many cuts through it. The resulting sections reveal a sequence of varying topography, as if one took cinema stills and flipped through them to animate movement across the land. Cinematic sectioning has been used to depict the complex site of the Eurhythmics Centre in Alicante, Spain. Through the notation one follows the rise and fall of land waves as they move under ramps, and the method also choreographs the movement of people on the ramps. From these and other large-scale movements the building is generated. Indeed, the overall undulation of the Centre is another fractal, this time one which mimics the surrounding mountains. So the landform building not only sprawls like a geological formation but is actually a microcosmic representation; an idea not far from the way in which a Chinese garden 'borrows the landscape'.

Cinematic sectioning is a method of controlling the design of very large structures and it was used by several groups who entered the Yokohama Port Terminal Competition in 1995, an important event for the new paradigm with Greg Lynn, Reiser + Umemoto and the winners, Foreign Office Architects (FOA), all producing interesting Nonlinear Architecture. The young team of FOA (Farshid Moussavi and Alejandro Zaero-Polo) worked previously for both Rem Koolhaas and Zaha Hadid and are connected to the Architectural Association in London, with all the apostolic succession this implies. It is no surprise that their entry pushes several ideas of Complexity Architecture – folding, superposition and bifurcation – a step beyond their teachers.

Their landscape-building for Japan is a long, low horizontal folded plate of steel that will undulate across the water. Its structural strength is provided by the self-similar folds and the gentle undulations of the plates – flowing forms which are obvious metaphors of the sea. Paradoxically, the hard surface resembles a dry desert. It could be a moonscape pockmarked by activities strewn about in a carefully careless way, chaotic compositional tactics that Koolhaas termed 'confetti' when he deployed them at the Parc de la Villette.

The multi-layered topography for Yokohoma achieves both diversity and unity, disjunction and continuity. The architects are looking for a seamless structure, an alternative to collage and radical eclecticism, with which to deal with difference; a system they describe as 'continuous but not uniform'. They achieve this, to a degree, by folding various functions into a continuous surface full of feedback loops of circulation. If built, the rich mixture of different uses may be hard to administer because the usual visual borders do not orient and divide different kinds of passengers. One can imagine international and local travellers arriving late for a ship and becoming mixed up together as they head for one of those eye-shaped folds that peer from one level to the next. These 'bifurcations', as the architects call them following the complexity paradigm, unite different levels. Importantly they do so with a smooth continuity, rather like the way origami folds unite a complex pattern into a single sheet of paper.

In contrast to Eisenman's staccato grammar, the grid, the fold

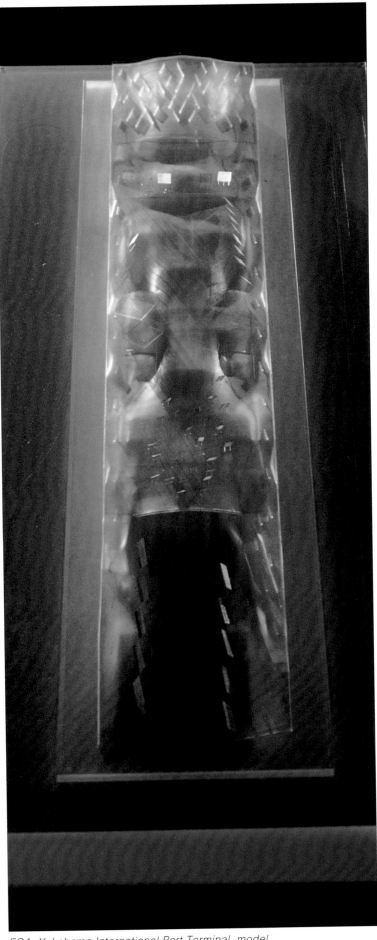

FOA, Yokohama International Port Terminal, model

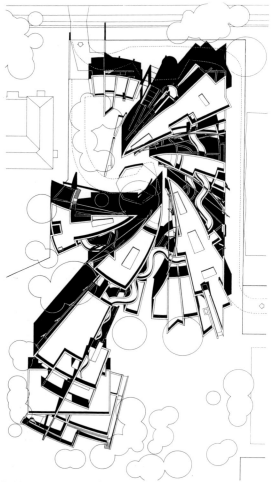

Zvi Hecker, Heinz-Galinski School, Berlin, 1993-95. Spiral sunflower geometry (anticlockwise) plus concentric curves plus grid generate complex landforms and self-similar curves and fish-shapes

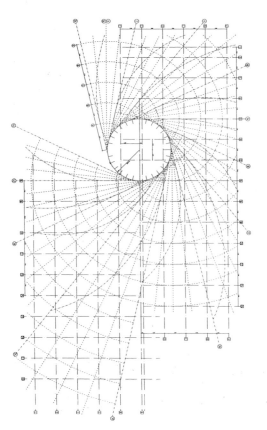

and undulation are employed in a soft way that blurs distinctions. One floor warps a bit of itself into another, producing a characteristic 'floor/door/window' and a sloping 'floor/ramp', the latter idea developed by Koolhaas. A challenge for architects today is to see if this idea can work better than it does at Frank Lloyd Wright's Guggenheim Museum.

As the model and sections indicate, this ferry terminal is a very abstract system, a landscape of otherness, a surprising flatscape without the usual orientation points; it does not look like a building at all. The generic nature of the scheme, the architects claim, is well-suited to our stage of globalised late-capitalism and, like Mies van der Rohe, they turn a universal system into a kind of transcendental space: a sacred space without a religion. Artificial land, second nature, has reached an apotheosis.

The fractal landform

If FOA, this time like Eisenman, prefers an abstract system to a representational one, then the Israeli architect, Zvi Hecker reverses the preconception with his Jewish school in Berlin. The Heinz-Galinski School creates an extended landform out of explicit metaphors. Snake corridors, mountain stairways, fish-shaped rooms are pulled together with an overall sunflower geometry. It sounds constricting, even Procrustean, but, on the contrary, the sunflower, with its spiral of movement towards a centre can generate a general order, especially, as here, when tied to two other geometries – the grid and concentric circles. The three systems, like Eisenman's tilts, make every room slightly different, or self-similar, and the sunflower spiral results in a very strong pull to the heart of the school (the architect, when he saw it from a helicopter, said it looked like 'a friendly meeting of whales'). Some will find this centrality too obvious, the imagery too readable and insistent, but again one is surprised by the generality and abstraction of the grammar.

This small institution for 420 pupils is the first Jewish school to be constructed in Germany for 60 years. Built in the leafy suburbs of Charlottenberg, it literally keeps a low profile – two to three storeys – and threads its sunflower geometry amid the existing trees. The most satisfying aspect is its urbanity. It creates tight curving streets, or walkways, which give a sense of mystery not unlike an historic town, where contingency has created the odd shapes and spaces. Here a restricted palette of grey concrete, silver corrugated metal and white stucco is interwoven with trees. Each of the three colours, as with Eisenman's pink, green, and blue, corresponds with a different geometric system. This allows contractors to understand and build a complex woven structure and also, of course, allows the complexity to be interpreted. The point is generally true of these landform structures. They depend on systematic logic, both for construction and orientation; not the simple logic of one grid, but three or four systems in tandem. Again, the contrast with Modern architecture is quite obviously that between complexity and simplicity, although it is not an absolute contrast. Here, for instance, simple materials, simple formulae and abstraction have generated the complexity.

Six of the sunflower petals curve counterclockwise around a circular green and one enters a void where the seventh might have been. This semi-public space, with its subtle mixture of cobbles and grass, metal and stucco, Jewish ruins and concrete, gives a strong sense of identity: the physical counterpart for the strong community life which goes on here. Part Torah school, part synagogue, part community facility with public meeting

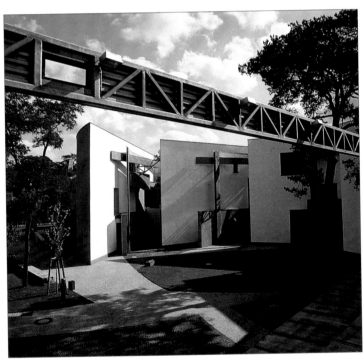

Heinz-Galinski School, Berlin

rooms, the Heinz-Galinski School has to play an ethnic role in Berlin which is not dissimilar to Libeskind's Jewish Extension to the Berlin Museum: it must fit in and yet be unmistakably other.

Several discreet signs, such as a Jewish star, are placed in the background and their presence is felt at the same level as the architectural symbolism; for instance, the plan of the six petals, which is also punched into the concrete. The latter becomes a decorative logo and explanatory map for new visitors. It also suggests the wider intentions of Hecker, which are to produce a cosmic order based on the omnipresent spiral form and, in particular, the solar dynamics of the sunflower. He has under-

lined the paradox of 'a wild project' that has 'very precise mathematical construction'. 'Above all', he notes 'is its cosmic relationship of spiral orbits, intersecting one another along precise mathematical trajectories.'[4] The mixture of an abstract system and a few discrete signs and images is finely balanced.

The group ARM (Ashton Raggatt McDougall) a Melbourne office, also reaches this balance in some of its post-modern buildings, and the opposition is usually a symbolic programme set against technical virtuosity. At Storey Hall in Melbourne, ARM has created one of the most exuberant expressions of the new paradigm. The building, on one of the main downtown streets of

ARM, Storey Hall, Melbourne, 1993-96. Fractal forms of window, doorway, bronze surface and metal cornice are based on the aperiodic tiling pattern derived by Roger Penrose – a new, always changing order for urbanism

Melbourne, is part of the highly urbanised campus of RMIT. Its explosion of green and purple fractals (with yellow and silver highlights) sends up its neighbours to either side. At the same time, like Gaudí's Casa Batlló with which it is comparable, it also makes subtle acknowledgements to these neighbours with its cornice line, window scale and basic tripartition. Basically, however, like Eisenman's Cincinnati addition, it is proposing a new urbanism, a new system which is a discrete shift from those of the past. No longer the classical ordonnance, no longer the boredom of Miesian curtain wall! Here is a different way of ordering the landscape which is more organic and chaotic than both the classical and modern systems. Potentially, if it were generalised as a whole street system, it could be just as harmonious as those of the past. Why doesn't some architect try it on a whole street – create the new subtle order of urbanism? The system awaits its Alberti.

At street level, Storey Hall presents a large green and purple doorway – quite a shock. The green folded plates of concrete blur into purple folds ('blurring', again as with FOA, is a favourite term of the architects, here likened to smeared lipstick). As justification Howard Raggatt cites the fact that green and purple were the heraldic colours of the previous inhabitants, Irish and feminist groups. In this and other ways, the building takes its cues from history, the typical post-modern method of building in time and historical depth.

Most evident are the patterns of bronze fractals – lozenge shapes, both fat and thin – that dance over the concrete surface. These are versions of the famous Penrose tiling pattern, which I will explain shortly, and they are self-similar to the doorway and other forms in metal: so the variety of shapes is harmonic, related and fractal, but hardly ever self-same (as in a Modernist building).

The bronze panels of the facade are articulated further by a green, linear meander, and the surface-squiggles look as if they were folds in a rock, or skin. Finally, to the left and on the *piano nobile* (to use the classical term of the adjoining buildings) is a linear part of the Penrose pattern, punched violently through the surface. The architect, Howard Raggatt, ironically quoting one of the responses to the building, speaks of this jagged void as if 'Roger Rabbit went through the concrete wall'; but significantly he sees the point of appropriating the unusual image through metaphor and popular culture.[5] He lists the variety and overlap of metaphors – 'broken vegemite jar, kryptonite building, gates of hell, Ivy League creeper, green house for leprechauns, the true geometry of space, from Plato's to Einstein's cave' – suggestive, contrary images which provoke different readings.

Inside the building the variegated themes are elaborated. A high entrance space breaks through several levels, surmounted by a twisting stair and is compressed to one side by the cave entrance. The first floor foyer is further compacted by three surfaces: large, abstracted fractals of the facade, folded plates of a bigger dimension. Finally, one reaches the auditorium, where the concentration of themes is even more intense.

The auditorium ceiling erupts overhead with the Penrose pattern – now in acoustic tile – that is at once reptilian and cave-like. The metaphor of an undulating skin is maintained, but developed to accommodate lighting and the requirements of music, drama and lectures. Here, and on the walls and stage, the fractal grammar is rendered in different scales and in opposite tastes. If Eisenman's system at Cincinnati is abstract, cool but Rococo, ARM's system is representational, hot and Art Deco. At a general level, both architects have used the computer to

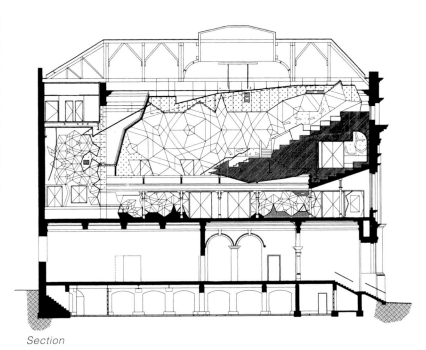

Section

generate a new grammar based on complexity theory, although because the structure of Storey Hall is old this cannot be elaborated in volume.

One of the most important contributions of the building is the development of the Penrose tiling pattern into an order that connects facade, floor, walls and ceiling into a single ornamental system. Roger Penrose, the Oxford mathematician, inventor and author, discovered a tiling pattern with five-fold symmetry that was previously thought to be impossible. Using a fat and thin rhombus, he created an aperiodic tiling system which, however far it is extended, never results in a cyclical pattern. This unusual, self-organising order was later in 1984 discovered to exist in nature. It was termed a quasicrystal, because it had an orientational but not translational order, whereas a crystal has both. Like a crystal it has a holistic order, but it also has a higher degree of complexity, since the pattern is everywhere slightly different. Quasicrystals, with a fractal self-similarity, are potentially more suited to architecture than the repetitive use of the square because they are not self-same – in a word, boring.

To recognise the Penrose enigma one has to break the pattern down into ten-sided decagons, which resemble faceted footballs. One begins to discover that each football overlaps with another on a thin rhombus. At Storey Hall a more emphatic supergraphics, a green linear pentagon, is laid over the decagons. The two rhythms then dance together in gentle syncopation, two distinct beats played off against each other. The result may be somewhat overbearing on the street, but in the foyer and auditorium it makes for appropriate, visual music.

Even if they have not answered it, the architects of Storey Hall have posed a very interesting question: what if a whole street were ordered this way, what if a new complexity grammar replaced the self-same rhythms of classicism and Modernism? What if the city grew like a quasicrystal, and an ever-changing order emerged which was never quite repeated?

The Japanese-based Ushida Findlay Partnership has not quite answered this question either, but also seeks a fractal urban order. This is based on continuous curves, such as the spiral. The Truss Wall House, Soft and Hairy House and House for the Millennium are more fluid and continuous than the other buildings illustrated here, because a monotone white surface unites all planes. It absorbs those elements – fixtures and windows – which are usually separated in colour and form. Katherine Findlay, who grew up on a Scottish farm, speaks of a fluid, rubbery architecture and, like Eisenman, she favours models such as the slime mould and metaphors taken from movement, because they represent flexibility, and activity close to the body.

Ushida Findlay Partnership, Truss Wall House, Tokyo, 1994. A spiral of movement generates self-similar curves in white continuity

Fluid fractals

No architect has yet reached this state of organic flexibility. The Surrealists proposed it in the 1920s and Salvador Dali admired Gaudí's works because they were viscous or, as he called it, 'edible architecture'. Frank Gehry, at the new Guggenheim Museum in Bilbao, has been approaching this fluidity; he has pushed the grammar he first developed at the Vitra Museum in more supple directions. Smooth, continuous forms in steel and limestone flow towards a centre point to erupt in a flower of petals. Where before at Vitra the units were distorted boxes, they are now more linear, smooth and continuous. The grammar has an all-over, seamless continuity like Ushida Findlay's work.

The new museum has the presence of a robust, urban plant. It might be a hardy bulb or bush pushing its way opportunistically through holes in the pavement. Tough, riotous, savage – sprouting against the odds, for light and life, it is the image of Gaia overcoming the harsh city hardscape, maybe even a weed thriving on toxic waste. No, it is too graceful for that, but the burgeoning energy is unmistakably present, erupting from below, climbing over the rectilinear structures like a creeper which cannot be suppressed. Actually, many of the gallery spaces are rectilinear – an effective contrast to what happens above – and one of them stretches under the high-speed motorway and bridge to reach up on the other side. This petal serves as another entrance. It also becomes another landform that ties the building into large-scale technology and the sprawl of the city, urban realities that are accepted not denied by this inclusive work.

Does any other building command an urban setting with such presence, indeed capture the landscape with such power? Chartres? The Acropolis? Ronchamp? These three sacral structures come to mind because they, too, stand out from the context and at the same time give the landscape a direction, even supporting role. When one sees the new Guggenheim from the surrounding hills, it seems like a silver magnet drawing a grey city together. Overpowering, resplendent, exuberant – a cathedral caught like Laocoon in the embrace of a slippery snake, trying to squeeze out. Metaphorical excess? Inevitable, when confronted by these glowing, exploding curves – a supernova of museum as cathedral, looking for worshippers who love the new science.

Actually, on a more pedestrian level, Gehry has related the museum to three city scales: that of the bridge, captured by an entry tower that snakes under it; that of the existing roof tops, whose heights are acknowledged by the atrium and lower forms; and the Bilbao River, an important historical waterway, which is taken into the scheme, both literally through large windows and the viscous, silvery forms.

To connect the museum to the city, Gehry has used a limestone (from Granada) which relates to the sandstone of adjacent structures. He has also designed a very large city space, an atrium even more powerful than New York's original Guggenheim, which also has a large expanding space at its centre. The Bilbao atrium does not have a function beyond orientation and thus it could be conceived as both a pure aesthetic space and public town square, opening out to the river. Aware that this relative freedom allowed him to upstage Wright at his own game of spatial gymnastics, Gehry says, only partly ironically, that he intends to have a holographic portrait of that wilful architect looking down on visitors – jealously, disapprovingly. Formally, the new atrium takes the exterior grammar and turns it inside out, so that the petal shapes compress inwards, and bend upwards with curved glass.

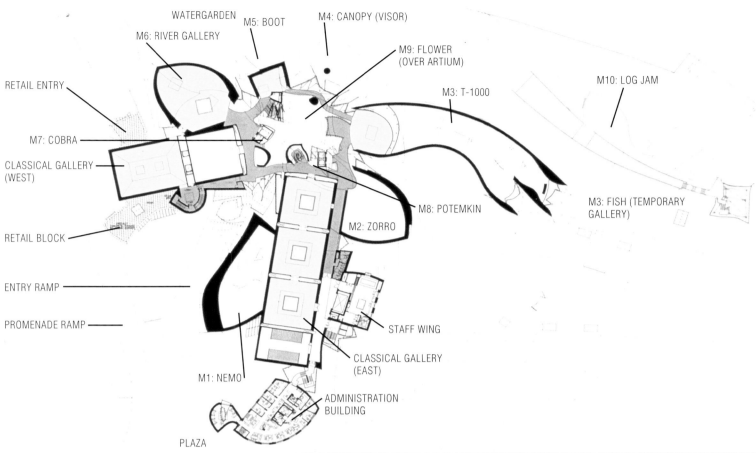

WATERGARDEN   M5: BOOT   M4: CANOPY (VISOR)

M6: RIVER GALLERY

M9: FLOWER
(OVER ARTIUM)

RETAIL ENTRY

M3: T-1000

M10: LOG JAM

M7: COBRA

CLASSICAL GALLERY
(WEST)

M8: POTEMKIN

M3: FISH (TEMPORARY
GALLERY)

RETAIL BLOCK

M2: ZORRO

ENTRY RAMP

PROMENADE RAMP

STAFF WING

CLASSICAL GALLERY
(EAST)

M1: NEMO

ADMINISTRATION
BUILDING

PLAZA

ABOVE AND OVERLEAF: Frank O Gehry, The Guggenheim Museum, Bilbao, Spain, 1993-97. Self-similar petals erupt in the centre and curl under the bridge, which ties the museum to contemporary technology and the urban landscape

The result is a new kind of ambiguous architecture, more folded on to itself than the glass box which introduced Modernist notions of transparency. Here are reflections of reflections and the self-similarity of crystals, the handling of glass facets and their intersections which causes a virtual image to splinter into many layered fragments. Views are partly veiled by walls of light that lead the eye up to the public ramps and roof terraces, which in turn give onto the urban landscape and river – making the museum a celebrant of the city.

While the Bilbao museum has a diversity of form and colour, what remains in the mind is the organising metaphor – the robust flower with its riotous petals blowing in the wind. There are approximately 26 self-similar petals, which reach out and come to a point which extends as a line. Just as light and shadow are sculpted by the flutes of a Doric column, so a shadow line is created by the pinched petals. The arris or fillet defines each volume in a much more supple way than at Vitra; perhaps this is a visual refinement, but it is also a clear example of the way that Gehry and the tradition he is in are learning step by step from their own work.

Like so many other buildings in the paradigm, this one has had the fat trimmed off by computer, using a program called 'Catia', developed by the French aeroplane manufacturer Dessault. The complex steel framing was kept to a minimum, as was the cutting of the masonry; necessary economising when dealing with curved buildings. There is always a lot of wastage when one carves from a block, unless the offcuts can be used or kept to the minimum. Gehry, like Grimshaw and others, has spoken of the way in which new computer software, designed for other technologies such as aircraft, can be used to cut the cost of fabrication by a large percentage. Here the Catia system has

worked out the volumes following a wood model and calculated exact dimensions as seen from any point, or any cut through a complex curve. These dimensions can be translated into the bent steel undersheets and then the pre-bent titanium cladding allowing all the tolerances to be worked out ahead of time in the factory. This cuts costs, but it results in the same size titanium panel throughout, a rigidity which I criticise elsewhere in this issue, because it is out of keeping with the general approach — that is, fractals, self-similarity, and varying the module to suit the curve and function.

Not inform but emergent form

The new complexity paradigm in architecture is evolving simultaneously in different directions. Landform buildings are perhaps the most prominent of the species, but they do share qualities with the others. One area of overlap is the concern for organic metaphors of design: the petals of Zvi Hecker and Frank Gehry, and the geological formations of Eisenman and Miralles. Another is the attempt to get closer to nature and its fractal language, as ARM and Ushida Findlay are doing. To some extent they are all producing an artificial landscape; a construction in-between the reality of the city, a building and the landscape.

There is more than one way to see these buildings, and the Spanish architectural critic, Luis Fernandez-Galliano, has seen them within a tradition of art that stems from the writings of Georges Bataille.[6] This French philosopher attacks the notion of hieratic form in architecture and proposes, instead, a 'formlessness' which several artists have sought. Yves-Alain Bois and Rosalind Krauss, in an exhibition at the Centre Pompidou entitled 'Inform', showed the kind of work that approaches formlessness. The dust and broken shards of Robert Smithson; the rusted,

rotted and collapsed forms of Lucio Fontana; the wasted forms of Robert Morris and Andy Warhol typify much of this work involved, as it is, with entropy. The problem of the art, aside from the fact that its predictability becomes boring, is that none of it is truly informal, formless or entropic. It is still very much 'pattern-making', even if of a minimal kind. It is hard to approach a condition of complete chaos, but computer programs can help our progress along this road if we want to travel it.

One of the few architects to use entropy in this way is Coop Himmelblau, who often composes buildings according to a method not far from throwing sticks into a random heap (as in the game of 'Pick-up-Sticks'). This, however, is not the method used by Eisenman, Libeskind, ARM or the others. Rather, they have used random means to allow an organisation to emerge; they have been very selective about the initial conditions – the fractal shape grammars – and the final stage of fine-tuning, that is, after a stage of random generation. In short, they do not pursue formlessness but emergent form, the *mutter* emerging from matter.

The intention may be the desire to get closer to the reality behind nature, the generative qualities behind both living and dead matter, that is, once again, the cosmogenic process which complexity theory has recently tried to explain. Representing emergence and creativity *per se* cannot be done, but it can be presented by an architecture that is as fresh and unlikely as one finds here.

BELOW: Inside the Guggenheim Museum curved glass walls compress into the space and layer it with the pinched arris so that reflections and transparencies are made even more ambiguous

Adapted from the last chapter of The Architecture of the Jumping Universe, *Revised Edition, Academy Editions (London), 1997*

Notes

1 The leading practitioners of Cosmogenic Design or Nonlinear Architecture or the Architecture of Emergence are Eisenman, Gehry, occasionally Koolhaas and the Organic-Tech architects. Certain buildings by Daniel Libeskind and Kisho Kurokawa fall into this tradition but were unfinished at the time of writing and so not discussed here. Other examples of Nonlinear Architecture in progress are Nicholas Grimshaw's Stock Exchange, Berlin and Kisho Kurokawa's Fukui City Art Museum.
Works that might have been illustrated in a longer discussion include Kijo Rokkaku's Budokan, Tokyo, 1990-93; Kathryn Gustafson's gardens in France; Günther Domenig's Stone House, Austria, 1985-95 and perhaps his Z-Bank; Nigel Coates' Penrose Institute, Tokyo, 1995; Philip Johnson's Monsta House, New Canaan, 1996; the roof structures of Japanese architects Coelcanth, Shoei Yoh, Hitoshi Abe and the sculptural projects of M Takasaki. In addition, there are the folded plate works of engineers Ted Happold and the Frei Otto group and the nonlinear structures of Cecil Balmond; the wooden structures of Herb Greene, Imre Makovecz and Bart Prince, and some of Reima Pietilä's work, especially the early Dipoli Centre and Kiillemoreeni.
Important theorists and designers who are developing the paradigm include Jeff Kipnis, Greg Lynn, Bahram Shirdel and Ben van Berkel. A very early work to explore the form language of folding and curves is Frederick Kiesler's Endless House, 1959, developed from his Endless Theatre of 1926.

2 Peter Eisenman quoted in Joseph Giovannini, 'Campus Complexity', *Architecture*, AIA Journal (Washington), August 1996, pp114-25.

3 Sanford Kwinter, 'The Genius of Matter: Eisenman's Cincinnati Project', in *Re:working Eisenman*, Academy Editions (London), 1993, pp90-97.

4 Zvi Hecker, quoted in pamphlet *Heinz-Galinski-Schule, Berlin, Aedes Galerie und Arckitekturforum*, January 1993, p14.

5 Howard Raggatt and ARM, 'New Patronage', from pamphlet *RMIT Storey Hall, Faculty of Environmental Design*, RMIT (Melbourne), 1996, pp8-9

6 Luis Fernandez-Galiano, 'Lo Informe', *Arquitectura Viva 50*, September-October, 1996.

FRANK O GEHRY

THE GUGGENHEIM MUSEUM
Bilbao, Spain

The site for the museum is in a prominent location at the edge of the river bank where the main vehicular bridge crosses it, between the Museo de Bellas Artes and the City Hall. It is very close to the major business district of the city which was created on a 19th-century street grid. Connections to the city via tree-lined walkways and public spaces, plazas and the river front promenade are emphasised in the scheme. Vistas from the city have been created so that the river is visible through the buildings.

The scale of the expressed building parts relates to the existing buildings across the road and river, while the height of the atrium roof relates to the adjacent roof tops. The tall tower at the east end of the scheme 'captures' the bridge and makes it part of the building composition. Bilbao's river has been very important in its history and this is reflected in the introduction of the large areas of water in the project.

The programme for this design requested a 30,000 square-metre world class, modern and contemporary art museum including three different types of exhibition space: permanent site and specific installations; and temporary exhibition galleries. Additionally, the design includes other public facilities such as a 400-seat auditorium, a restaurant, a café, retail space, and a large central atrium/orientation space which was envisioned to function almost as a public town square. Loading, parking, support, storage and administrative office space is also included but because of the unique nature of the collection, the proportion of front-of-house to back-of-house space is about 2:1, as opposed to a more normal ration of 1:2.

The programme of the museum is distributed on the site in several interconnected buildings, with a large central atrium space with its figural roof unifying the composition. Parking and back-of-house support facilities are located on the lowest levels adjacent to the truck dock and freight elevators.

The entry plaza leads into the central space which is surrounded on all four levels by galleries and has a large glass wall facing on to the river. Ramps and stairs provide access to the roof terraces where there are views out over the river and city. The external circulation also provides opportunities for routing large crowds during 'blockbuster' shows outside the flow of normal circulation.

Gallery spaces are articulated as large rectangular volumes stacked upon one another, some of up to 30 metres width at the east end under the tall tower and column free space. Skylights are provided via the sculptural roof forms above the temporary exhibition gallery building and a shaft through the west gallery. Gallery ceiling heights are generally maintained at six metres or more.

The auditorium is located on the entry plaza so that it can be used independently or as part of the museum. A restaurant is located at the north-west corner of the site overlooking the river and a café is located by the river walk.

The major materials for the gallery buildings are limestone and sandblasted stainless steel, both of which are available locally. The structure is a composite of concrete and steel frame with a tense ring created to hold the atrium roof together. Mechanical systems are designed to maintain appropriate levels of control for the various uses. An access floor is used throughout the gallery space to allow flexibility for the infrastructure.

Lighting will be a combination of indirect ambient light; direct exhibition light from a flush flat monopoint system; and filtered daylight from skylights and windows.

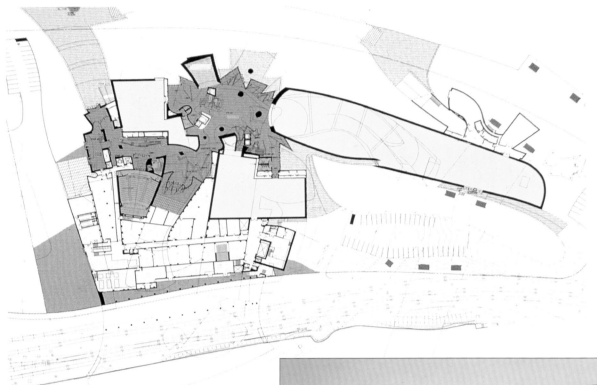

ABOVE: First floor plan; BELOW: Computer-generated perspectives

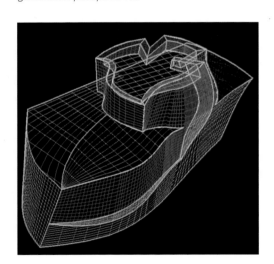

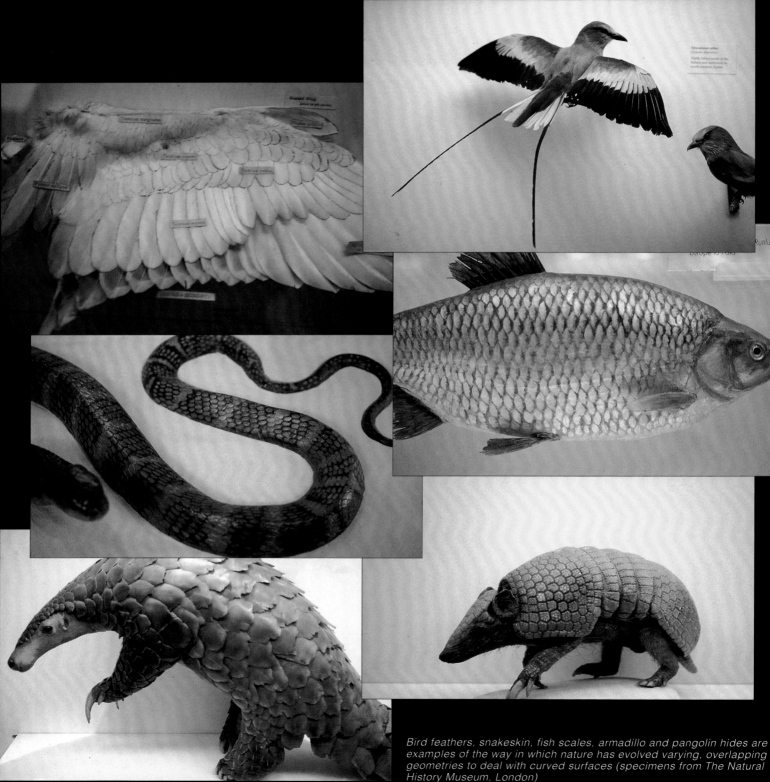

Bird feathers, snakeskin, fish scales, armadillo and pangolin hides are examples of the way in which nature has evolved varying, overlapping geometries to deal with curved surfaces (specimens from The Natural History Museum, London)

THE SURFACE OF COMPLEXITY
THE WORK OF FRANK O GEHRY
Charles Jencks

Several issues are clarified as new architectural grammars evolve. Whereas Peter Eisenman is pushing that of the folded plate and the staccato cube (broken flat form), Frank Gehry, in the recent projects shown here, is advancing the vocabulary of undulating surfaces. The developments of Greg Lynn and Shoei Yoh (blob grammar) lie somewhere in-between and one can imagine several other morphological types (ice or crystal facets, rock accretions, bubble and muscle systems) as well as more random ones.

Oddly enough, since his fish lamps of 1983, Gehry has decreased the variety of the fish scales: instead of the scales, or shingles, varying with increased curvature as they go around a tight bend, they have tended towards repetition. The same metal shingle is repeated again and again at the Vitra Headquarters (1989-92), and the Guggenheim Museum, Bilbao (1992-97), and continues to be in the most recent projects. Why – economy? With computer design and production, is it really much cheaper to repeat than vary? The skin of a building is a small percentage of the costs.

Another issue raised by Gehry's recent undulations is the question of 'poche' – unusable, left-over space; the space between the curves and some of the interior rectangular spaces. It strikes me that there are two unexploited areas here: to layer shingles of varying size so that they bring out the exponential curves and, secondly, to develop *transparent*, layered surfaces so that the contrast of rectangle and curve, inside and outside, can be heightened.

Two notions – the scaling of fractals, which Benoit Mandelbrot emphasises, and the exposure of inner workings – have been experimented with in Gehry's previous work but they have never been developed fully as methods of expression. Perhaps we will see this happen; these ideas fall out of the curved grammar and someone is sure to create new architecture out of the possibilities.

Section of Samsung Museum of Modern Art, South Korea, 1996

The Guggenheim Museum, Bilbao, 1992-97

Model of Samsung Museum of Modern Art, South Korea, 1996: the rectangular shingle at a large scale is pinched and given an edge arris to accentuate the linear flow of forces

Model of Berlin Conference Room, Pariser Platz 3, 1995: the rectangular shingle over a 'horse head' diminishes towards the mouth and folds towards the eye

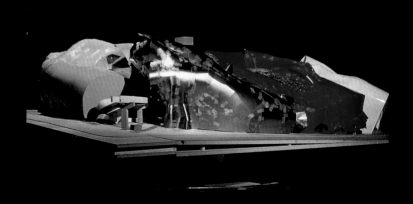

Model of Experience Music Project Museum, 1996: the rectangular shingle sometimes tightens around severe eruptions and sometimes is laid atectonically – a blob of architecture with the occasional arris giving it visual strength

Model of Chiat House, Telluride, Colorado, 1997: again the large, rectangular shingle is undulated at a big scale and given edge fillets to let in light – lava plus crystals

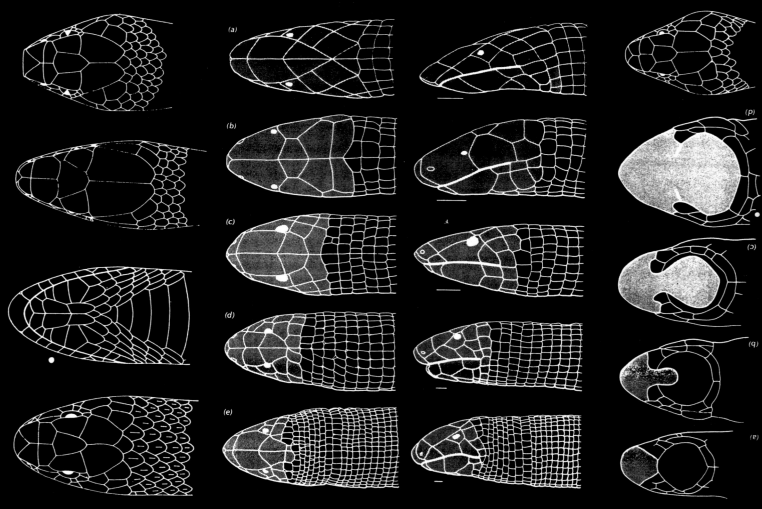

Details of snake scales

ASHTON RAGGATT McDOUGALL

STOREY HALL

Melbourne

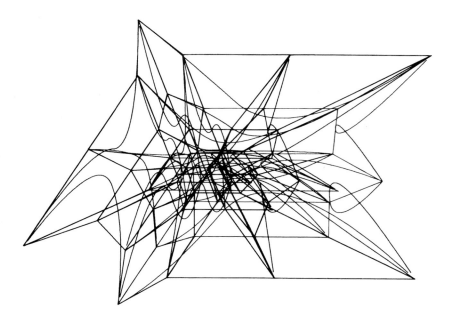

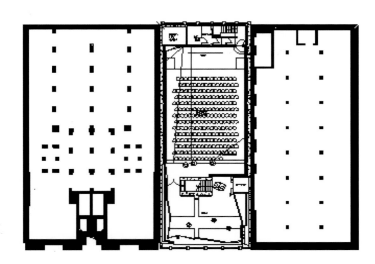

FROM ABOVE: Straight lines and splines superimposed; ground floor plan

To everybody's astonishment it turned out that the three-dimensional forms of these tiles may underline a strange new kind of matter. *Roger Penrose*

Blurred zone

Naturally enough our design did not begin with Roger Penrose's famous non-periodic tile, nor even with tiles at all. Instead, our ongoing thematic was the condition of the blur, of a zone necessitating a continuous means of exacting precision; a zone notoriously popping out of focus, as if becoming smeared, becoming fast, or as if projected into a kind of systematic digression, necessarily duplicitous, or of preconceived judgements, preconceived interpretation, a kind of inconsolable discipline of intuition, as if, and even if always, under the turgid rigours of a somehow unholy exegesis.

We began by almost literally stretching old Storey Hall along the street to designate a zone for the new annex, documenting that blur on the open topped copier, slipping the photograph by hand. Inevitably and necessarily watching, we were momentarily blinded by brilliant light, as if having a vision, pretending, face glowing, like one who has seen God, one who has noticed a crack in the discourse of cause and effect, if only for a moment, as though knowing that longing, documenting that stutter in space and time, that new matter, now, according to Einstein, or as pictured by Pollock, now hanging suspended, almost permanently signifying that which is no longer simultaneous, no longer inexorably rooted to that causality, now blurred by that vital strangeness, that longing, no longer wholly articulate, like a cry from afar, like voices in that ancient cave, with those monstrous shadows of dancers still flickering, still projected by fire, but as if now transfigured, as if according to

Rabbinic tradition suggesting more of the 49 levels of meaning assigned to the exegesis of revealed text, presumably foundations un-exhumed, now no longer determined by commonsense, struggling to find a role for real latency, explicit premonitions as on the lips of those with slurred speech, the blurred talk of those drunk with deciphering or even listening to that awful voice again, speaking freely, as if no longer requiring translation, as if we stood once again in another city, Ur, again, much as Abraham had, listening to that voice telling us to pack our bags, our tents, our loved ones, our sheep and our asses to follow the blur to another promised land, another pentateuch of five-fold symmetries, once the 'forbidden symmetries', as Penrose calls them, but now underlying that 'strange new kind of matter.'

Exacting pixelation
Inevitably, mere construction of the blur necessitates exacting means of definition, the search for the operations of which have tried the satisfaction of our efforts. Exacting by pixelation, by the zeros and ones, made visible in 256 colours, 65,536 tones, then 16,777,216 before the step to true colour, test the acuity of our eye, its definition of smooth curves, as of the shadow, always a matter of scale, of magnification, of testing the virtue of thresholds.

Gradually, the Penrose Tile became for us, both outside and in a means of deep pixelation, two tiles, zero and one, no longer merely surface, but popping into space, taking ornament with it and making it structure, self supporting, self generating, as if inventing its own rules of displacement in advance, as if conscious of its own prefigurations, as if in possession of its own X and Y chromosomes, slivers of infinite surface like sections of solid space, an infinite knot of non-repetition, of lines which cannot be navigated, 'no matter how much of it you explore you can never determine which tiling you are on . . . it is no help to travel far out and examine disconnected regions, because all the regions belong to one large finite region that is exactly duplicated infinitely many times on all patterns'.

Einstein's cave: a green knot
Somehow from the very beginning of this project to implant the new auditorium in its neo-classical host we had a kind of vision simulation of a place hidden, or a place still waiting, like imaging the interior bubble of an unbroken amethyst

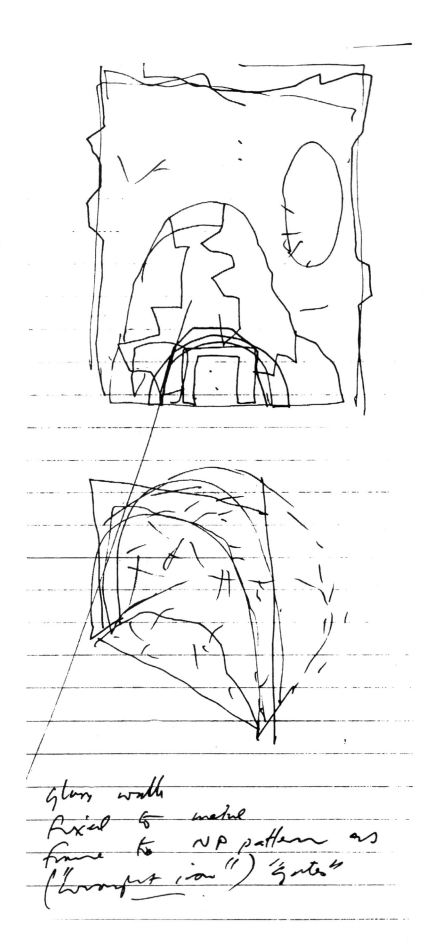

glass walls
fixed to metal
frame to NP pattern as
("transition") "gates"

Conceptual sketch

boulder, mottled green and purple sparkling or like standing in a magnificent imagined space without light, now absolutely black and pressing on eyes and face, eyes bulging without light, the space trembling like the just-in-time landscape of an arcade game, always rushing towards the cusp of a flickering emerging space, just as the pixels find definition, just as the previous moment vanishes or is otherwise transformed, stuttering in real time again, at that crack in causality, perhaps exposing the structures of our amusement, just before it snaps together and we race forward glowing, into zones just before recognition, zones of continuous connotation, almost *precise*, almost *predestined by real-time contingency*, dependent now only on the instantaneous point of view, on an embrace of abandoned objectivities, remaining always as background, mostly watched by peripheral vision, necessarily just out of focus, before the freeze frame or the End Game.

So just as the dancers around the fire in Plato's cave remained unseen to those watching their phantasmagorical shadows over the craggy interior surface, arousing theoretically analogous speculation on the nature of pure forms, now Einstein's cave conjures another analogous circus for our watching minds.

THE NEW AGE OF THE ORGANISM
MAE-WAN HO

Organic space-time *versus* mechanical space-time

O
rganic space-time *versus* mechanical space-time
I am told that the comet in our sky visited us 4,000 years ago. As it revolves once around the heavens, earth has revolved 4,000 times around our sun, and human beings have gone from stone age to space age in 160 life cycles. The comet looks like a giant eye in the sky, now within our orbit and looking down on us, having seen, perhaps, many other worlds in far-flung reaches of the universe during its space odyssey. Do any of those other worlds contain beings that gaze back at it as we do? One begins to get a sense of a multitude of space-times entangled with our here and now. The here and now contains in its essence a myriad of there and thens. That is the real sense in which the 'fullness of time' is to be understood. It is the reality of organic space-time that the mechanistic world-view has flattened out of existence.

Mechanical space and time are both linear, homogeneous, separate and local. In other words, both are infinitely divisible, and every bit of space or of time is the same as every other bit. A billiard ball *here* cannot affect another one *there*, unless someone pushes the one here to collide with the one there. Mechanical space-time also happens to be the space and time of the commonest 'common-sensible' world in our mundane, everyday existence. It is the space-time of frozen instantaneity abstracted from the fullness of real process, rather like a still frame taken from a bad movie-film, which is itself a flat simulation of life. The passage of time is an accident, having no connection with the change in the configuration of solid matter located in space. Thus, space and time are merely coordinates for locating objects. One can go forwards or backwards in time to locate the precise objects at those particular points. In reality, we know that we can as much retrace our space-time to locate the person that was 30 or 50 years younger as we can undo the wrongs we have committed then. There is no simple location in space and time.[1]

Psychoanalyst-artist Marian Milner[2] describes her experience of 'not being able to paint' as the fear of losing control, of no longer seeing the mechanical common-sensible separateness of things. It is really a fear of being alive, of entanglement and process in the organic reality that ever eludes mechanistic description. And yet, it is in overcoming the imposed illusion of the separateness of things that the artist/scientist enters into the realm of creativity and real understanding – which is the realm of organic space-time. Mechanical physics has banished organic space-time from our collective public consciousness, though it never ceases to flourish in the subterranean orphic universe of our collective unconscious and our subjective aesthetic experience. In a way, all developments in Western science since Descartes and Newton may be seen as a struggle to reclaim our intuitive, indigenous notions of organic space-time, which, deep within our soul, we feel to be more consonant with authentic experience.

Organism versus mechanism

The mechanistic world-view indeed officially ended at the beginning of this century. Einstein's relativity theory broke up Newton's universe of absolute space and time into a multitude of space-time frames each tied to a particular observer, who therefore, not only has a different clock, but also a different map. Stranger still – for Western science, that is, as it comes as little surprise to other knowledge systems, or to the artists in all cultures – quantum theory demanded that we stop seeing things as separate solid objects with definite (simple) locations in space and time. Instead, they are delocalised, indefinite, mutually entangled entities that evolve like organisms.

The profound implications of this decisive break with the intellectual tradition of previous centuries were recognised by a mere handful of visionaries. Among them, the French philosopher Henri Bergson,[3] and the English mathematician-philosopher Alfred North Whitehead.[4] Between them, they articulated an organicist philosophy in place of the mechanistic. Let me summarise some of what I see to be the major contrasts between the mechanical universe and the universe of organisms.

Mechanical Universe	Organic Universe
Static, deterministic	Dynamic, evolving
Separate, absolute space and absolute time, universal for all observers space-time frames	Space-time inseparable, contingent observer (process)-dependent
Inert objects with simple locations in space and time	Delocalised organisms with mutually entangled space-times
Linear, homogeneous space and time	Nonlinear, heterogeneous, multi-dimensional space-times
Local causation	Non-local causation
Given, nonparticipatory and hence, impotent observer	Creative, participatory; entanglement of observer and observed

The contrasts are brought into sharper relief by considering the differences between mechanism and organism, or, more accurately, the opposition between a mechanical system and an organic system. First of all, a mechanical system is an object *in* space and time, whereas an organism is, in essence, *of* space-time. An organism creates its own space-times by its activities, so it has control over its space-time, which is not the same as external clock time. Secondly, a mechanical system has a stability that belongs to a *closed* equilibrium, depending on controllers, buffers and buttresses to return the system to set, or fixed points. It works like a non-democratic institution, by a hierarchy of control: a boss who sits in his office doing nothing (bosses are still predominantly male) except giving out orders to line managers, who in turn coerce the workers to do whatever needs to be done. An organism, by contrast, has a dynamic stability, which is attained in open systems far away from equilibrium. It has no bosses, no controllers and no set points. It is radically democratic, everyone participates in making decisions and in working by intercommunication and mutual responsiveness. Finally, a mechanical system is built of isolatable parts, each external and independent of all the others. An organism, however, is an irreducible whole, where part and whole, global and local are mutually implicated.

I hope you are sufficiently persuaded that we need a radically new way of understanding the organism, if not the whole of nature, as Whitehead intimates. In this project, we – each and everyone of us – are especially privileged, because we are ourselves organisms and know in intimate, exquisite detail, what it is to be alive.

The vast majority of scientists as well as the general public have remained untouched by this conceptual revolution. Quantum theory itself sits uneasily and paradoxically between the necessary limits of a mechanical description (in quantum *mechanics*) and the elusive, organic reality that remains ever out of reach. Mathematics and physics have recently broken out of the strict mechanistic mould to explore the 'organic' realm (see Ho[5, 6] and Saunders, this volume pp48-53). In mathematics, computations have made accessible previously intractable problems in nonlinear dynamics, fractal geometry and chaos. In the meantime, physics has witnessed an astonishing inventory of empirical successes – high temperature superconductivity, quantum coherence and nonlocal quantum superposition of states – even as theoretical descriptions have lagged far behind. It is precisely at the point where theoretical description fails to capture the organic freedom of reality that contemporary science is at its most captivating. It is the realm of imagery where scientist and artist meet, and where no one who is not both can enter.

The end of mechanistic biology
Mainstream biology is left far behind. It is clinging fast to the mechanistic era. The discovery of the DNA double-helix in the late 1950s, which has made its permanent mark on the public consciousness, was the climax to a century of mechanistic, reductionist biology – the idea that the whole is the sum of its parts, that cause and effect are simply related, and can be neatly isolated. The discovery ended the quest for the material basis of the units of heredity – the genes – that are supposed to determine the characters of organisms and their offspring, thus firmly establishing the predominance of the genetic determinist paradigm. The subsequent flowering of molecular biology gave rise to the present era of recombinant DNA research and commercial genetic engineering biotechnology.

What few people realise is that the very successes of recombinant DNA research have completely undermined the foundations of the genetic determinist paradigm, at least ten years ago. There has indeed been a revolution in genetics which exactly parallels the transition between mechanical and quantum physics. The new genetics signals the final demise of mechanistic biology, and is consonant with the diametrically opposite, organicist perspective which has been emerging in the rest of science. The contrast between the old, pre-recombinant DNA genetics and the new genetics is presented below.

The Old Genetics	The New Genetics
Genes determine characters in a linear, additive way	Genes function in a complex, nonlinear, multidimensional network – the action of each gene ultimately linked to that of every other.
Genes and genomes are stable and except for rare random mutations, are passed on unchanged to the next generation	Genes and genomes are dynamic and fluid, they can change in the course of development, and as the result of feedback metabolic regulation
Genes and genomes cannot be changed directly in response to the environment	Genes and genomes can change directly in response to the environment, these changes being inherited in subsequent generations
Genes are passed on vertically, i.e. as the result of interbreeding within the species, each species constituting an isolated 'gene pool'	Genes can also be exchanged horizontally between individuals from the same or different species

The parallel to the transition from classical to quantum physics is best illustrated by focusing on the concept of the 'gene'.[7] In the old genetics, the 'gene' is a continuous stretch of DNA, with a particular base sequence, and a constant, simple location in the

Energy Flow

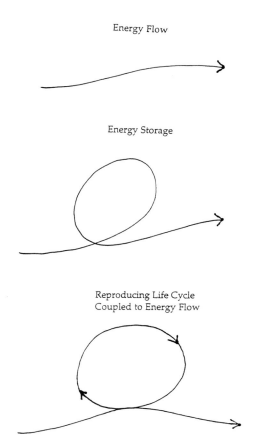

Energy Storage

Reproducing Life Cycle
Coupled to Energy Flow

Figure 1. *Energy flow, energy storage and the reproducing life cycle*

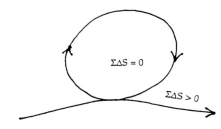

$\Sigma \Delta S = 0$

$\Sigma \Delta S > 0$

Figure 2. *The many-fold cycles of life coupled to energy flow*

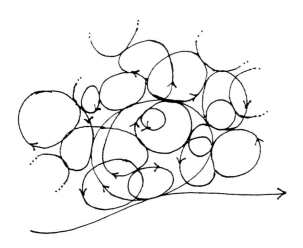

Figure 3. *The organism frees itself from the immediate constraints of thermodynamics*

genome, that specifies, via a non-overlapping triplet code, the amino-acid sequence of a single protein. The amino-acid sequence of the protein, in turn, determines its function in the organism. The genetic code is universal, and there is a 'one-way information flow' from DNA to an intermediary 'messenger' RNA to the protein, and no reverse information flow is possible. This was the notion of a definite, isolatable gene, specifying a function independently of the cellular and environmental context.

The cracks in the old edifice first appeared when *reverse* information flow was found to occur from RNA back to DNA. Then, the genetic code was discovered to be overlapping and non-universal. Next came a succession of revelations showing that the gene itself has no well-defined continuity nor boundaries, the expression of each gene being ultimately dependent on, and entangled with every other gene in the genome. Far from the one-way information flow that is supposed to proceed from DNA to RNA to protein and on to the rest of the organism, gene expression is subject to influences and instructions from the cellular and environmental contexts. The gene can be recoded, or edited by the cell, it can get silenced, or converted to a different sequence. Genome organisation is infinitely variable, dynamic and fluid. Genes mutate frequently, small and large rearrangements take place, genes jump around, sequences are added or deleted, they get amplified thousands and hundreds of thousands of times or they get contracted. These changes may take place as part of normal development or they occur repeatedly in response to environmental challenges. Some of the genetic changes are so specific that they are referred to as 'directed mutations' or 'adaptive mutations'. Genes can even jump horizontally, by infection, between species that do not interbreed. Genes and genomes are in reality, dynamic, delocalised, mutually entangled and part of larger wholes. In short, biology has been catapulted, over the heads of the old guard, into the new age of the organism.

I have given a good indication of what the new 'physics of the organism' might look like in an earlier book[8] and in other recent publications.[9] In the rest of this paper, I shall outline a theory of the organism, ending with a few remarks on certain key aspects that are most relevant to organic, as opposed to mechanistic forms: organic stability, organic space-time and the integral delocalisation of organic forms.

A theory of the organism
There are 75 trillion cells in our body, made up of astronomical numbers of molecules of many different kinds. How can this huge conglomerate of disparate cells and molecules function so perfectly as a coherent whole? How can we summon energy at will to do whatever we want? And most of all, how is it possible for there to be a singular 'I' that we all feel ourselves to be amid this diverse multiplicity and plurality?

To give you an idea of the coordination of activities involved, imagine an immensely huge superorchestra playing with instruments spanning an incredible spectrum of sizes from a piccolo of 10^{-9} metres up to a bassoon or a bass viol of 1 metre or more, and a musical range of *72 octaves*. The amazing thing about this superorchestra is that it never ceases to play out our individual songlines, with a certain recurring rhythm and beat, but in endless variations that never repeat exactly. Always, there is something new, something made up as it goes along. It can change key, change tempo, change tune perfectly, as it feels like it, or as the situation demands, spontaneously and without hesitation. Furthermore, each and every player, however small, can enjoy maximum freedom of expression, improvising from moment to moment, while maintaining in step and in tune with the whole.

I have just given you a theory of the quantum *coherence* that underlies the radical wholeness of the organism. It is a special wholeness that involves total participation, and maximises *both* local freedom and global cohesion. It involves the mutual implication of global and local, of part and whole, from moment to moment. It is on that basis that we can have a sense of ourselves as a singular being, despite the diverse multiplicity of parts. That is also how we can perceive the unity of the here and now, in an act of 'prehensive unification'.[10] Artists like scientists, depend on the same exquisite sense of prehensive unification, to see patterns that connect apparently disparate phenomena.

In order to add corroborative details to my story, however, I shall give a more scientific narrative involving some easy lessons in thermodynamics and quantum theory. It begins with energy relationships.

The thermodynamics of organised complexity

Textbooks tell us that living systems are open systems dependent on energy flow. Energy flows in together with materials, and waste products are exported as well as the *spent* energy that goes to make up *entropy*. And that is how living systems can, in principle, escape from the second law of thermodynamics. The second law, as you may know, encapsulates the fact that all physical systems run down, ultimately decaying to homogeneous disorganisation when all useful energy is spent, or converted into entropy. But how do living systems manage their anti-entropic existence?

I have suggested[11] that the key to understanding how the organism overcomes the immediate constraints of thermodynamics is in its capacity to store the incoming energy, and in somehow closing the energy loop within to give a reproducing, regenerating life cycle (see Figure 1). The energy, in effect, goes into complex cascades of coupled cyclic processes within the system before it is allowed to dissipate to the outside. These cascades of cycles span the entire gamut of space-times from slow to fast, from local to global, that all together, constitutes the life-cycle (see Figure 2 for an intuitive picture). Each cycle is a domain of *coherent* energy storage – coherent energy is simply energy that can do work because it is all coming and going together, as opposed to incoherent energy which goes in all directions at once and cancel out, and is therefore, quite unable to do work.

Coupling between the cycles ensures that the energy is transferred directly from where it is captured or produced, to where it is used. In thermodynamic language, those activities going thermodynamically *down*-hill, and therefore yielding energy, are coupled to those that require energy and go thermodynamically *up*hill. This coupling also ensures that *positive* entropy generated in some space-time elements is compensated by *negative* entropy in other space-time elements. There is, in effect, an internal energy conservation as well as an internal entropy compensation. The whole system works by reciprocity, a cooperative give and take which balances out over the system as a whole, and within a sufficiently long time. The result is that there is always coherent energy available in the system. Energy can be readily shared throughout the system, from local to global and *vice versa*, from global to local, which is why, in principle, we can have energy at will, whenever and wherever it is needed. The

organism has succeeded in gathering all the necessary vital processes into a unity of coupled non-dissipative cycles spanning the entire gamut of space-times up to and including the life-cycle itself, which effectively feeds off the dissipative irreversible energy flow (see Figure 3).

But how can energy mobilisation be so perfectly coordinated? That is a direct consequence of the energy stored, which makes the whole system *excitable*, or highly sensitive to specific weak signals. It does not have to be pushed and dragged into action like a mechanical system. Weak signals originating anywhere within or outside the system will propagate throughout the system and become automatically amplified by the local energy stored, often into macroscopic action. Intercommunication can proceed very rapidly, especially because organisms are completely *liquid crystalline*.

The liquid crystalline organism

Several years ago, we discovered an optical technique that enables us to see living organisms in brilliant interference colours generated by the liquid crystallinity of their internal anatomy. We found that all live organisms are completely liquid crystalline – in their cells as well as the extracellular matrix, or connective tissues.[12] Liquid crystals are states of matter between solid crystals and liquids. Like solid crystals, they possess long-range orientation order, and often, also varying degrees of translational order (or order of motion). In contrast to solid crystals, however, they are mobile and flexible and highly responsive. They undergo rapid changes in orientation or phase transitions when exposed to weak electric (or magnetic) fields, to subtle changes in pressure, temperature, hydration, acidity or pH, concentrations of inorganic molecules or other small molecules. These properties happen to be ideal for making organisms, as they provide for the rapid intercommunication required for the organism to function as a coherent whole. Some images of live organisms taken from video-recordings are shown in figure 4.

What you are seeing is the whole of the organism at once, from its macroscopic activities down to the long-range order of the molecules that make up its tissues. The interference colours generated depend on the structure of the particular molecules, which differ for each tissue, and their degree of coherent order. The principle is exactly the same as that used in detecting mineral crystals in geology. But, with the important difference that the living liquid crystals are *dynamic* through and through, as the molecules are all moving about busily transforming energy and material in the meantime. So, how can they still appear crystalline?

Because visible light vibrates much faster than the molecules can move, the tissues will appear indistinguishable from static crystals to the light transmitted, *so long as the movements of the constituent molecules are sufficiently coherent*. Actually, the most actively moving parts of the organism are always the brightest, implying that their molecules are moving all the more coherently. With our optical technique, therefore, one can see that the organism is thick with coherent activities at all levels, which are coordinated in a continuum from the macroscopic to the molecular. That is the essence of the organic whole, where local and global, part and whole are mutually implicated at any time and for all times. These images draw attention to the wholeness of the organism in another respect. All organisms – from protozoa to vertebrates without exception – are polarised along the anterior-posterior axis, or the oral-adoral axis, such

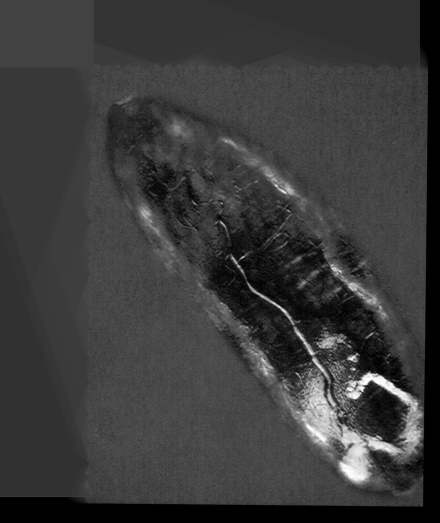

Figures 4a, 4b

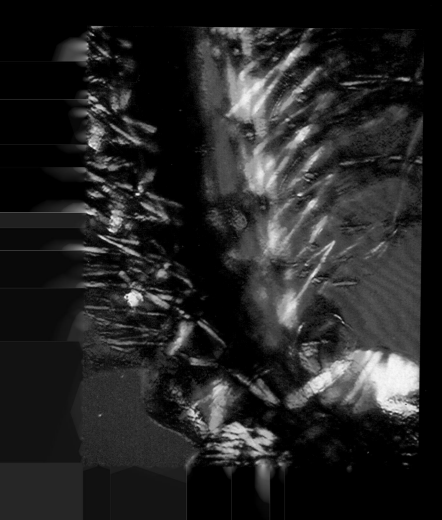

that all the colours in the different tissues of the body are at a maximum when the axis is appropriately aligned in the optical system, and they change in concert as the axis is rotated from that position. The fruitfly larva has cleverly demonstrated that for us by curling its body around in a circle (figure 4 c,d).

The coherence of organisms and nonlocal intercommunication
As I said before, intercommunication can proceed very rapidly through the liquid crystalline continuum of cells and connective tissues that make up the organism. In the limit of the *coherence time* and *coherence volume* of energy storage – the time and volume respectively over which the energy remains coherent – intercommunication is instantaneous or nonlocal. There is no time-separation within the coherence volume, just as there is no space-separation within the coherence time. Because the organism stores coherent energy over all space-times, it has a full range of coherent space-times, which are furthermore, all coupled together. Thus, there is a possibility for nonlocal intercommunication throughout the system. In the ideal, the system is a quantum superposition of coherent activities, constituting a 'pure coherent state' that maximises both local freedom and global cohesion, in accordance with the *factorisability* of the quantum coherent state.[13] Factorisability means that the different parts are so perfectly intercorrelated that the intercorrelations resolve neatly into products of the self-correlations. So the parts behave as though they are independent of one another. This is the radical nature of the organic whole (as opposed to the mechanical whole), where global cohesion and local freedom are both maximised, and each part is as much in control as it is sensitive and responsive.

The 'whole' is thus a domain of coherent activities, constituting an autonomous, free entity,[14] *not* because it is separate and isolated from its environment, but precisely *by virtue of its unique entanglement of other organic space-times* in its environment. In this way, one can see that organic wholes are nested as well as entangled individualities. Each can be part of a larger whole depending on the extent over which coherence can be established. So, when many individuals in a society have a certain rapport with one another, they may constitute a coherent whole and ideas and feelings can indeed spread like wildfire within that community. In the same way, an ecological community, and by extension, the global ecology may also be envisaged as a superorganism within which coherence can be established in ecological relationships over global, geological space-times.[15]

The ideal quantum coherent state involving the whole system is a global *attractor* to which the system tends to return when it is perturbed, but as the system is always open, it will invariably be taken away from the totally coherent state. So here is how space-time, as well as entropy or time's 'arrow', is generated.[16] It is generated in proportion to the *in*coherence of actions taken. The more the actions taken are at odds with the coherence of the system, the more time, and entropy, is generated, and the more the system ages. Thus, the biological age of an organism may literally be quite different from the age as measured by external clock-time. In the same way, the earth itself can be ageing much faster on account of our incoherent actions within it. On the othe

The liquid crystalline organism: still frames from a video-recording of live organisms viewed with a special polarised light microscopy technique which detects liquid crystalline regimes – figures 4a, 4b, successive frames of a first instar fruitfly larva about to hatch; figures 4c, 4d successive frames of the first instar fruitfly larva shortly before hatching

hand, we may indeed enter a state of delocalised timelessness when we achieve a high degree of coherence. Some of us get an inkling of that during an aesthetic experience, or alternatively, a religious experience.

Several people have asked me whether it is possible to get younger. My first reaction was no, because for all real processes, according to the textbook, entropy is greater than or equal to zero. On further reflection, however, I think the answer has to be yes. It follows from the principle of internal entropy compensation in an organic system, where negative as well as positive entropy can be generated, and also because past and present, as well as present and future, can be *nonlocally* interconnected. The challenge is indeed to set ourselves and the earth back on a possibly rejuvenating, or at any rate, anti-entropic and self-sustaining course.[17]

Organic space-time and fractal space-time

Organic space-time is tied to activity, and as elaborated above, these activities are fundamentally anti-entropic on account of their tendencies towards coherence. The organism is thus a coherent space-time structure engendering nonlocal interconnectedness. What is the nature of this structure?

There are several lines of recent evidence converging to a new picture of the 'texture of reality'[18] suggesting that organic space-time does have a structure, and that this structure is fractal. One of the most exciting discoveries in recent years, which has given rise to the science of complexity is that natural processes and natural structures have *fractal* dimensions. That means they have dimensions in between the one, two or three to which we are accustomed. Fractals capture a new kind of order characterised by self-similarity – the similarity of part to whole over many different scales. Snowflakes, clouds, ferns, coastlines, branching patterns of blood vessels, and the 'cytoskeleton' inside each cell are all examples of fractal structures. Natural processes, from weather patterns to the healthy heart-beat and electrical activities of the brain, similarly, exhibit 'chaotic dynamics' that when spatialised as a 'Poincaré section'[19], gives rise to 'strange attractors' that again have fractal dimensions. If space-time is indeed generated by processes as I have proposed here, then it should also exhibit fractal dimensions, or more accurately, multi-fractal dimensions. This is the basis of the 'space-time differentiation' of organisms.[20]

According to Nottale[21] and others, the whole of present day physics relies on the unjustified assumption of the differentiability of the space-time continuum, which stems from the classical domain, whereas Feynman and Hibbs[22] have already shown that the typical path of a quantum particle is continuous, but *non*differentiable. This is the failure of present-day physical description to capture the organic quantum reality that I have alluded to earlier; for the description is still based on a mathematical representation of space-time as continuous and homogeneous, i.e. as infinitely divisible or 'differentiable'. It so happens that a structure that satisfies the requirement for continuity and non-differentiability is also fractal. Nottale writes:

> Giving up the hypothesis of differentiability has an important physical consequence: one can show that curves, surfaces, volumes and, more generally, spaces of topological dimension D_T, which are continuous but non-differentiable, are characterized by a length, an area and, more generally a D_T measure which becomes explicitly dependent on the resolution at which they are considered . . . and tends to infinity when the resolution

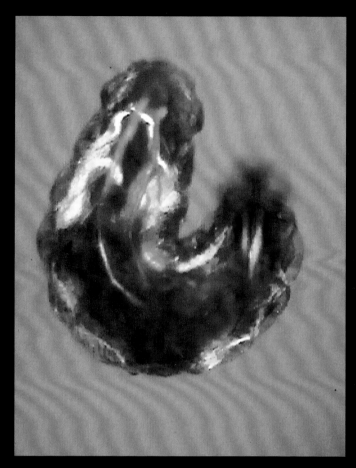

Figures 4c, 4d

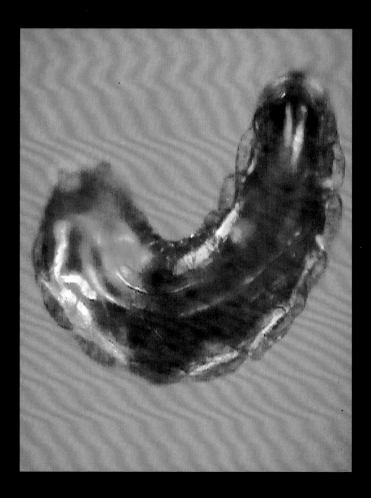

interval *e* tends to zero. In other words, a non-differentiable space-time continuum is necessarily fractal . . . This result naturally leads to the proposal of a geometric tool adapted to construct a theory based on such premises, namely, fractal space-time.[23]

The author then proceeds to describe a new approach that generalises Einstein's principle of relativity to scale transformations. Specifically, the equations of physics are required to keep their form under scale transformation, i.e. to be scale covariant. It allows physicists to recover quantum mechanics as mechanics on a fractal space-time, in which Schrödinger's wave equation is a geodesic equation.

I wonder if that is not the beginning of an approach towards the quantisation of space-time which, I believe, is a necessary consequence of the quantisation of action that Planck's constant already involves. This quantised space-time is also Bergson's 'duration', which expresses the indivisible multiplicity of our subjective experience of organic process.[24] It is the experience of processes cascading through the continuous scales of fractal space-times that are all coupled together or entangled through the coherence of the 'ground' or asymptotic state, over which the scale covariance is defined.

What would an organic architecture be like?

Organic architecture is nothing new. As Jencks points out, '"Organic unity, where not a part can be added or subtracted except for the worse" are injunctions that have rebounded through the halls of building sites for 2,000 years.'[25] The artists have been well ahead of scientists after all. Jencks touches on some of the themes developed in this chapter in his grand panoramic sweep of how the new 'science of complexity' is changing architecture and culture. However, as with quantum theory itself, much of the science of complexity is still mechanism aspiring towards organism. So, perhaps there is an excuse for me to give in to the temptation of trying to imagine what organic architecture would be like, based on the new view of the organism just presented, and to make connections with some well-known and lesser known concepts in established organic architecture.

Organic stability versus mechanical stability

One question which arose (for some of us) in the wake of the discoveries of the new genetics is, how do organisms and species maintain their stability when genes and genomes are so mutable and fluid? That is a question on the nature of organic stability in general.

The conventional, neo-Darwinian explanation is that natural selection is always at work to select out those that are unstable, and hence 'unfit', so only those that are sufficiently stable remain to propagate offspring like themselves. A neo-Darwinian account of architecture, might similarly explain that buildings are selected for stability – those that were not stable simply fell down and eliminated themselves, leaving the stable ones for us to admire and to imitate.

I do not know how that explanation fares in architecture, but it certainly fails to account for the responsiveness of organisms, including their genes and genomes, to environmental and physiological changes.[26] The stability of organisms and species is dependent on the entire gamut of dynamic feedback interrelationships extending from the socio-ecological environment to the genes. Genes and genomes must also adjust and respond, and if

necessary, change, in order to maintain the stability of the whole. As stated above, the stability of organisms is diametrically opposite to the stability of mechanical systems. Mechanical stability – which includes that of so-called 'cybernetic' systems – belongs to a closed, static equilibrium, maintained by the action of controllers, buffers or buttresses designed to return the system to set points. Organic stability, on the other hand, is a dynamic balance attained in open systems far away from equilibrium, without controllers or set points, but by means of intercommunication and mutual responsiveness. The stability of organisms depends on *all* parts of the system being informed, participating and acting appropriately in order to maintain the whole.

Organic stability is therefore delocalised throughout the system, via symmetrically commuting parts, each of which changes in response to all the others and to the environment. I am reminded of Cecil Balmond's constructions (see this volume), his 'free forms' which defy gravity. Organic stability is in the dynamic integrity of the whole. I can imagine the stresses and strains distributing and ever-shifting from one part to another in cycles of correlated reciprocity. If these forms were made of transparent, liquid crystalline material, as living organisms are, one might see a beautiful display of ever-changing colour patterns reflecting the shifting patterns of stresses and strains, as the structure communicates with its environment, just as one can see in real organisms.

Organic forms are supported and sustained by their relationship to the environment. Liquid crystals, in particular, are constantly evolving embodiments of their changing environments, their surfaces are invariably curved and flexible, hence the study of their structure is referred to as 'flexi-crystallography' by crystallographer Alan MacKay. Liquid crystals go through many abrupt phase transitions, each 'phase' being itself a continuum of more subtle variations. The phases are all minimum energy surfaces separating an 'inside' from the 'outside', though the inside and the outside can be so thoroughly interdigitated that it becomes a major problem in topology to disentangle them. The infinite variety of intricately sculpted exoskeletons of radiolarians are mineral deposits templated by different liquid crystalline formations. Liquid crystalline structures have already inspired certain architectural designs, such as the carpark in the National University of Mexico.[27]

Organic space-time and organic architecture

Whereas a mechanical form is located *in* space and persists (or not) in time, an organic form, by contrast, *is* a space-time structure; to be exact, a coherent space-time structure. An organic form *creates* space-time, increasing its space-time differentiation in the course of development and in evolution. Being *in* an organic form is to partake of its distinctive space-time, and its possibility for nonlocal interconnections over multiple dimensions. Jencks points out that virtually all those who referred to 'organic architecture', including classicists such as Vitruvius and Alberti, and modernists, such as Gropius and Wright, insisted on work that shows fractal self-similarity, or 'unity with variety'.[28]

I have proposed above that organic space-time *is* fractal because it arises out of natural processes which are fractal. Fractal architecture, therefore, is a unique creation of organic space-time that extends and enhances our experience as organisms. I am captivated by Bruce Goff's plan of his Bavinger House.[29] It exhibits the dynamic, nonlocal inter-connections and the multiple resonances of the fractal, organic whole, simultaneously unfolding and enfolding, diverging and converging in the gesture of life itself. I imagine sounds taking on added dimensions of musicality and coherence within this structure.

Another aspect of organic space-time is its complexity, or space-time differentiation.[30] This corresponds, I think, to Jencks' concept of the 'organizational depth' of an architecture – the 'density with which things are linked' – which counters the 'depthless present' of modernist architecture by 'building in time'. The depth of organic space-time is not just a nestedness but a special kind of superposition and entanglement. A fine example of space-time entanglement is Rem Koolhaas' library in Jussieu University, Paris.[31] It is a continuous linear route traversing a stack of near-horizontal planes connecting one level to the next; the whole floor is one unbroken multi-level ramp through which weaves 'a grid of columns and randomized incidents'.[32]

Of course, organic architecture is not restricted to fractal constructions, just as organic processes can undergo global phase transitions or catastrophic changes. In terms of space-time structure, phase transitions would correspond to major reorganisations of the system, giving rise to a new Schrödinger's wave or 'geodesic' equation. Jencks has explored nonlinear and catastrophic forms to much effect in his interior and exterior designs and in landscaping.

The integral delocalisation of organic forms and organic architecture

Finally, it must be stressed that an organism is an unique embodiment of its environment, that arises out of an uninterrupted act of 'prehensive unification',[33] a Bergsonian duration. Put in another way, the organism is an unique, integral space-time entangling a multitude of space-times. It simultaneously creates its own space-time while being constitutive of other space-times. As a work of art, the organic architecture is more than an icon or a symbol. It is a coherent superposition and entanglement that gives nonlocal access to the diverse multiplicity of space and times that constitute its integral whole. That may be the real challenge to organic architecture.

Bioelectrodynamics Laboratory, Open University, Walton Hall, Milton Keynes, MK 7 6AA UK.

Acknowledgments

This essay benefited from stimulating discussions with Charles Jencks and Cecil Balmond, and with Alan Mackay. Philipe Herbomel drew my attention to Nottale's papers on fractal space-time by kindly sending the xerox copies. Part of this article was first presented as a public lecture 'A theory of the organism and organic space-time' at a Conference on Time and Timelessness, Dartington Hall, April 9-13, 1997. I was much inspired by the occasion, by the responses of the audience, and by composer and scholar, Edward Cowie, who introduced my lecture. Julian Haffegee exercised great skill in preparing the colour images of figure 4.

Notes

1 A N Whitehead, *Science and the Modern World*, Penguin Books (Harmondsworth), 1925.

2 M Milner, *Not Being Able to Paint*, Heinemann Education Books (London) 1957.

3 H Bergson, *Time and Free Will. An Essay on the Immediate Data of Consciousness* (F L Pogson, trans), George Allen & Unwin Ltd (New York), 1916.

4 A N Whitehead, op cit.

5 See M W Ho, *The Rainbow and the Worm, The Physics of Organisms*, World Scientific (Singapore), 1993.

6 See M W Ho, 'The biology of free will', *Journal of Consciousness Studies* 3, 1996, pp231-44.

7 For details of this refer to M W Ho, *Genetic Engineering Dreams or Nightmares. The Brave New World of Bad Science and Big Business*, Third World Network (Penang), 1997.

8 M W Ho, *The Rainbow and the Worm, The Physics of Organisms*, op cit.

9 M W Ho (ed), *Bioenergetics, S327 Living Processes*, Open University Press, (Milton Keynes), 1995.
— 'Bioenergetics and the coherence of organisms', *Neural Network World* 5, 1995, pp733-50.
— 'The biology of free will', *Journal of Consciousness Studies* 3, op cit.
— 'Bioenergetics and biocommunication', in *Computation in Cellular and Molecular Biological Systems* (R Cuthbertson, M Holcombe and R Paton, eds) World Scientific (Singapore) 1996, pp251-64.

10 A N Whitehead, *Science and the Modern World*, op cit.

11 In M W Ho, 'The biology of free will', op cit; and 'Bioenergetics and biocommunication', op cit.

12 See M W Ho, 'Bioenergetics and biocommunication', op cit; and S Ross, R Newton, Y M Zhou, J Haffegee, M W Ho, J P Bolton and D Knight, 'Quantitative image analysis of birefringent biological material', *Journal of Microscopy*, 1997 (in press); and M W Ho, J Haffegee, R Newton, and S Ross (1995) 'Organisms are polyphasic liquid crystals' *Bioelectrochemistry and Bioenergetics* 41, pp81-91.

13 M W Ho, *The Rainbow and the Worm, The Physics of Organisms*, op cit; 'The biology of free will', op cit; 'Bioenergetics and biocommunication', op cit.

14 See M W Ho 'The biology of free will', op cit.

15 See M W Ho, *The Rainbow and the Worm, The Physics of Organisms*, op cit; and M W Ho, 'On the nature of sustainable economic systems', *World Futures*, 1997 (in press).

16 See M W Ho, *The Rainbow and the Worm, The Physics of Organisms*, op cit.

17 See M W Ho, 'On the nature of sustainable economic systems', *World Futures*, op cit.

18 See I Stewart, *Does God Play Dice: The Mathematics of Chaos*, Basil Blackwell (Oxford) 1989.

19 Ibid.

20 See M W Ho, *The Rainbow and the Worm, The Physics of Organisms*, op cit.

21 L Nottale, 'Scale relativity and fractal space-time: applications to quantum physics, cosmology and chaotic systems', *Chaos, Solitons and Fractals* 7, 1996, pp877-938.

22 R P Feynman and A F Hibbs, *Quantum Mechanics and Path Integrals*, MacGraw-Hill (New York), 1965.

23 L Nottale, 'Scale relativity and fractal space-time: applications to quantum physics, cosmology and chaotic systems', op cit.

24 See M W Ho, *The Rainbow and the Worm, The Physics of Organisms*, op cit.

25 C Jencks, *The Architecture of the Jumping Universe*, Academy Editions (London), 1995; chapter VIII, 'Self-similarity (fractals) and strange attractors' p43.

26 See M W Ho, *Genetic Engineering Dreams or Nightmares. The Brave New World of Bad Science and Big Business*, op cit.

27 Alan Mackay, personal communication.

28 C Jencks, *The Architecture of the Jumping Universe*, op cit, p43.

29 Ibid, p45.

30 See M W Ho, *The Rainbow and the Worm, The Physics of Organisms*, op cit.

31 See C Jencks, *The Architecture of the Jumping Universe*, op cit, p87.

32 Ibid, p88.

33 A N Whitehead, *Science and the Modern World*, op cit.

NONLINEARITY

WHAT IT IS AND WHY IT MATTERS

PETER T SAUNDERS

Modern science was founded on the assumption that the universe runs according to a small number of simple laws which humans can discover and understand. The task of the scientist is to find these laws and to work out how they combine to produce all the different phenomena that we observe. Explanations of highly complicated phenomena may fall short of this ideal, but they are generally considered to be inferior, which is why physics and chemistry are 'hard' sciences, while biology is a 'soft' science.

The 18th-century French mathematician, Laplace, once claimed that if he were told the position and momentum of every particle in the universe at a single instant in time, he could predict the entire future and reconstruct the whole of the past. I doubt that anyone has ever believed this could really be done, but it has defined the project: everything should be explained in terms of the lowest possible level and ultimately in terms of the motions of individual particles obeying Newton's laws.

Of course this world view did not begin with Newtonian mechanics. It is a part of European culture that goes back to the mathematics of the Greeks and to the Old Testament tradition of a single deity who dictated a book of laws for his chosen people to interpret and obey. A Talmudic scholar and a theoretical physicist have a lot in common. But it was given a tremendous boost by Newton and his successors, who created an enormously successful science based on it.

The influence of the Newtonian paradigm has been felt outside physics as well. The theory of evolution by natural selection is not based on Newton's laws, but its claim to account for the whole of the living world in terms of a single mechanism places it firmly within the paradigm; Darwin is indeed the Newton of the grass blade. Karl Marx claimed to have discovered the laws of motion of society. Modern scientists have similar ambitions: the goal of sociobiology is to base the social sciences on the principles of population genetics.[1]

Ironically, physicists themselves no longer believe in the solid, deterministic, clockwork universe that gave such support to the paradigm. In its place they have created a world in which space and time depend on the observer, in which certain properties exist only when we measure them, in which one part of the theory insists that particles that are far apart cannot communicate instantaneously and another part contains results that cannot be explained unless they do, and so on.

Despite all this, the Newtonian paradigm has survived almost unscathed. This is partly because few people outside nuclear physics really understand exactly how deep the problems are, and partly because however strange the quantum universe may be, it could be that the everyday world is largely unaffected, that the problems are all smoothed out by the law of large numbers. We may draw on the new physics occasionally, for example if we believe that quantum uncertainty in the brain is the source of free will, but that need not affect the general thrust of our research.

How far such a view is justifiable remains to be seen.[2] Besides, while we may well be able to study, say, economics without explicit reference to quantum mechanics, it must be unsatisfactory to restrict ourselves to a world view which is no longer accepted within the subject that is most responsible for its present dominance. If physics is to be the model for all science, it should be the physics of today, not of the 19th century.

In any case, the Newtonian paradigm is now faced with a challenge from a totally different direction. The problems arise because the universe is nonlinear, which we have always known, and that this matters, which is only now becoming clear.

Some of the properties of nonlinear systems have been understood for a long time; the mathematical analysis of the straw that broke the camel's back goes back to Euler in 1744. The modern subject began with a paper published by the great French mathematician Henri Poincaré in 1890, just before the appearance of relativity and quantum mechanics. The full impact has only recently been recognised, however, because it required new mathematical tools and, above all, powerful computers that allow us to explore nonlinearity in a way that was previously impossible.

Briefly, the message of nonlinear dynamics is this. Even if we restrict ourselves to Newtonian mechanics, we find that the world is not as the Newtonian paradigm would lead us to believe. In the first place, we could predict the future course of the universe from its present state only if we were given the data with infinite accuracy. Anything less than that, and the Laplacian project fails utterly. Second, nonlinearity endows systems with many properties which previously we thought had to be imposed on them by external forces. Phenomena that appeared to require special explanations can now be seen as no more than what we might expect. The universe is just like that. Why it should be like that is another question, but it is.

Nonlinear dynamical systems

Dynamical systems theory is the study of processes in motion, and since most processes are nonlinear, it is in effect the study of how most things behave. More precisely, and this is why it is a nontrivial subject, it's the study of the difference between how most things behave and how we suppose they behave if we don't think carefully enough.

The obvious meaning of linearity is having to do with straight lines, and since the equation of a straight line is $y = a + bx$, which has no powers of x or y higher than the first, linearity also implies that a system is describable by very simple equations, with no squares, products of variables, or anything else at all complicated. Mathematicians do use the word in that sense, but for them the most important meaning is additivity. A system is said to be linear if the sum of two solutions is a solution; in other words, if the total is precisely the sum of the parts.

To see why linearity in the usual sense is related to being able to add solutions, think of the simplest nonlinear operation: squaring. As you learned at school, you can't get the square of a sum by doing the squarings separately and adding the results: if $z = x+y$ then it is not true that $z^2 = x^2 + y^2$. There is a bit more to come, $2xy$ in case you've forgotten. And squaring is a particularly simple example: there's no sensible way of writing $\log(x+y)$ as $\log x + \log y$ plus a simple term in x and y.

The great advantage of linear systems is that they are relatively easy to analyse. Because we can add solutions, we can break a problem down into manageable bits, solve each of them separately, and then add everything up at the end. Even if the system isn't actually linear, the method may give the answer as accurately as we need or, if it doesn't, it may at least provide a first approximation which can be improved. This is a very powerful technique, and it has produced a lot of good science, but it doesn't always work. Above all, it is not appropriate for dealing with phenomena that arise directly out of nonlinearity.

Everyone knows the Earth is round, but you don't have to bother about this if you are planning a garden or even a city. With a much larger region, like the Canadian province of Saskatchewan, you have to be a bit more careful. When the pioneers were moving in, the government had the southern part of the province divided into square counties. Because the lines of longitude on a sphere are not parallel, the squares don't fit exactly, and you can see on a map of Saskatchewan that the counties on the borders with Alberta and Manitoba have had to be made a slightly different shape. With this minor adjustment, the basic linear plan still works.

If, however, Christopher Columbus had thought the Earth was flat, no minor adjustments to his charts would ever have suggested to him that he could get to the East by sailing west. The fact that you can travel around a sphere is an essentially nonlinear property, and we will not discover it by a process of successive approximations starting from a linear model.

This can be a serious problem for mathematical modelling, because it is not always easy to tell whether a system has important nonlinear properties. The classic example of the power of Newtonian mechanics is the calculation of planetary orbits. The theory predicts these should be very nearly elliptical, which is indeed what is usually observed. The point of Poincaré's famous paper was to show that this need not always be the case, and it has recently been verified by computer that very complicated orbits can exist within our own solar system. This is probably the reason there are gaps in the asteroid belt: the orbits of small bodies at that distance from the sun eventually move out of the region.

The assumption of linearity is at its most insidious when we aren't using mathematics at all, however. It creeps in because so much of our intuition is based on our own and other people's experience of the most intensively studied systems, which are linear. Most of the time, we tacitly assume that the whole is essentially the sum of the parts, that large effects must have large causes, and so on.

Of course we have all heard about the straw that broke the camel's back, and we all know that a stitch in time saves nine, but we see these as occasional exceptions to the general linear rule. They do not occur in the most commonly used mathematical models, which makes them seem less plausible – less respectable one might say. Besides, it is one thing to write down a nonlinear mathematical model and analyse it carefully; to introduce sudden jumps and thresholds on a purely *ad hoc* basis is generally unconvincing, to say the least.

As nonlinear dynamics becomes better understood, we will become more accustomed to the idea that the characteristic features of nonlinear systems can and do occur, so they will become part of our intuition. We will also learn where they fit in and where they do not. Without a detailed mathematical model, we may not be able to prove that a sudden jump must occur at a certain stage, or that a certain shape will appear, but we often can explain why we would expect it, why it is consistent with the rest of what is going on at the time.

Paradoxically, the two most characteristic features of nonlinear systems are chaos and order, each occurring where we might not have expected it.

Chaos

For mathematicians, the term 'chaos' does not imply total disorder. Instead, they mean what they call 'deterministic chaos', which sounds like a contradiction in terms, but is not. The behaviour is deterministic in that it has no inherently random element: in principle (and sometimes in practice too) we can write down the equations of motion and solve them. The chaos arises because the system is so sensitive to perturbations that even the slightest disturbance can rapidly build up into a major effect.

Now just about everything in real life is subject to perturbations. We can never specify the conditions precisely at the beginning, and there will always be disturbances along the way. So while we may be able to predict the behaviour of a chaotic system for a while, the small errors and perturbations rapidly build up to the point where the process may appear totally random. This is the hallmark of deterministic chaos: short-term predictability (because it is deterministic) together with long-term unpredictability (because it is so sensitive).

A familiar example is the weather. The Meterological Office has a very complex and detailed mathematical model of the Earth's atmosphere. They get reports from weather stations all over the world, and with these as starting values they solve the differential equations on a very powerful computer. This enables them to forecast the weather quite accurately for about a week in advance.

Now you might think that if they could keep increasing the number of weather stations and the power of their computer, they could extend the forecasts as far as they want. In fact, this isn't so. The system is chaotic, and even the smallest errors build up so rapidly that it is generally accepted that the practical limit is at most three weeks.

This is not because the atmosphere of the whole Earth is a large and complicated system. If that were the reason, then this would be nothing more than an extension of the obvious idea that it's not easy to make predictions about large, complicated systems.

In fact, the study of deterministic chaos began with the work of a meteorologist, Edward Lorenz.[3] He was working before powerful computers were available, and so he was studying just one small part of the system. Even that was beyond the capability of his computer, so he had simplified the model down to three very simple equations which he believed – rightly, as it turned out – captured the essence of what was going on:

$$dx/dt = -10x+10y \qquad dy/dt=28x-y-xz \qquad dz/dt=-(8/3)x+xy$$

Whether you understand differential equations or not, you can see that there are only two nonlinear terms, the two products xz and xy. So systems don't have to be very large to be chaotic, they also don't need to be very nonlinear. If large systems are more likely to exhibit chaos, it is mostly because the more subsystems there are, the more likely it is that at least one of them is chaotic.

But while weather forecasting beyond a couple of weeks or so may not be possible, we can still say something about what will happen. We can, for example, be quite confident that on the first day of the new millennium the temperature at noon in London will not be over 30°C. We don't need the Met Office's computer to know that; it comes from our experience of the climate in England.

If we did solve the equations on a computer, we would almost certainly end up with a prediction of a temperature between, say, 0 and 30, but it wouldn't be reliable, on account of the chaos. So

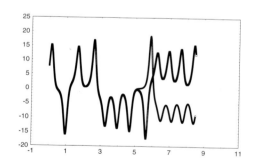

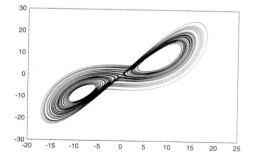

Figure 1. *Computer graph of Lorenz's equations: x against t (above); y against x (below)*

one result wouldn't be of any use. The best thing to do would be to run the program many times, using slightly different starting values each time. If we did this often enough we would build up a picture of the probability distribution of the temperature. But this would be no better than what we could have obtained far more easily from looking at past records.

You can see the effect in Figure 1, in which Lorenz's equations have been solved on a computer. The upper graph is a plot of x against t. The integration has been done twice, using different starting values of x that differed by less than 0.1 per cent. As you can see, the solutions are quite complicated, and while they stay together for a while, by the end there is no obvious correlation between them.

The lower graph is a plot of y against x. In contrast to the other one, this has a reasonable degree of order, even if the trajectory is a bit complicated. What is more, if you let the system run long enough, then no matter what starting values you choose, to within the resolution of the graph plotter you get the same figure, although it will be built up in a different order. This is why you've almost certainly seen this picture before, though not the one above it. There is order within the chaos.

Thus in addition to short range predictability and long range unpredictability, we also have a very stable long range predictability but only of some general features, not of the whole process. Thus in the midst of the first of one of the typical signs of nonlinearity, chaos, we see the other one, order.

Some properties of nonlinear systems

We can see the difference that nonlinearity can make by thinking of the familiar example of simple algebraic equations. The linear equation $ax+b=0$ has exactly one root (unless $a=0$) and it is real. The quadratic equation, $ax^2+bx+c=0$, has two roots, which may be real or complex. Thus when we move from linear to quadratic two things change. First, we no longer have a unique solution. Second, the solution can be an entirely new sort of object, a complex number.

If we get such significant changes with just a little bit of nonlinearity, you might ask what a lot more will do. The answer is, not much: there may be more than two roots, but that's about it. The roots are still either real or complex; there's nothing more exotic to come. Much the same is true of nonlinear dynamical systems. There doesn't have to be much nonlinearity before the important new features appear. This is why it is possible to study some carefully chosen simple nonlinear systems and have some confidence that we know what they are like in general.

While linear systems have at most a single equilibrium point, nonlinear systems typically have more than one equilibrium state and these can include trajectories as well as points. There are often bifurcation points, and also transitions from one stable trajectory to another, i.e. large changes on a very short time scale. Indeed, large changes usually happen in this way; the stability of the trajectories prevents small perturbations from accumulating.

To see what this amounts to in non-technical language, you can think of a system at a stable equilibrium like a ball at the bottom of a cup. If you disturb it, it goes back to its original position, but apart from that, it doesn't actually do anything. And indeed, linear systems in general are pretty limited, unless someone pushes them.

A system on a stable trajectory is more like a bobsleigh travelling down a run. Far from just sitting still, it is in motion all the time. It, too, can recover from being disturbed, but it doesn't go back to where it was; it picks up the track further down. To complete the picture, you have to imagine that there are typically several runs close together, so that if the bob hurtles out of one it may well land in another and finish its descent at a different end point. You have also to imagine that there are also forks, where one run splits into two and the driver can choose which branch to take. Even this doesn't fully describe what can happen, but at least you can see that nonlinear systems are much richer than linear ones. What is more, much of what happens depends on properties of the system itself (the layout of the runs, in the metaphor) and not on the external forces.

1. Biological development

Over half a century ago, the biologist CH Waddington was struck by some properties that seemed common to all developing organisms.[4] The process is stable: embryos do not need an absolutely perfect environment in which to develop and they can survive many small disturbances and even some large ones. If they are disturbed, development does not stop until they recover. Instead, they gradually return to the normal developmental pathway. Embryos do not have to be genetically identical to develop into very similar organisms. Apart from minor details, however, organisms tend to come in separate kinds; there are discrete species and varieties, not a continuous spectrum of types.

We can now see why developing organisms have these properties: it is simply because they are complex nonlinear systems. That is not to say that we should take organisms and their properties for granted, of course not. It is certainly wonderful that there are such things as organisms. On the other hand, once we know that there are such things as organisms, we should not be surprised that they have these properties. It is hard to imagine how they could be otherwise.[5]

2. Punctuated equilibria

The majority of evolutionists has always insisted that evolutionary change is gradual – in Darwin's words, *Natura non facit saltum*. If the fossil record shows discrete types with no intermediate forms, that is only because the record is incomplete.

About 20 years ago, however, Eldredge and Gould[6] put forward the theory known as punctuated equilibria. They claimed that the gaps in the fossil record are real, and that on the whole evolution proceeds not steadily but in rapid bursts, with long periods in between in which very little happens. This provoked a considerable controversy, with people writing about 'Evolution by Jerks' on the one hand and 'Evolution by Creeps' on the other.

It is not hard to see why. Neo-Darwinists (i.e. modern Darwinists) hold that evolutionary change occurs in the following way: random genetic mutations occur, some of these lead to changes in the phenotype (i.e. in the organism itself), and if these happen to be advantageous they are selected.

The theory locates the origin of the change in the genes, whereas selection acts on the phenotype. Neo-Darwinists seldom say anything about the connection between the two, but they implicitly assume that it is linear. A large change in the organism must have been caused by a large change in the genome. What is more, if the change in the genome is random, that in the organism must be random as well. Since it is totally implausible that the large genetic change required to bring about a significantly different but viable organism could occur by chance, evolutionary change *must* be gradual.

When we take nonlinearity into account, the whole picture changes. Because nonlinear systems typically have multiple equilibria and stable trajectories, we would not expect that major changes will occur as long sequences of minor ones. Instead, we would expect organisms to remain more or less unchanged for a long time and for large changes to occur rapidly as the developmental system moves to an alternative trajectory. Thus punctuated equilibria, far from being an awkward observation to be explained away, is precisely what we would expect to observe.

Self organisation

Nonlinear systems are capable of self-organisation, they can spontaneously generate order. For example, if water in a shallow tray is gently heated from below, the warmer water at the bottom will soon start to rise, while the cooler water at the surface will descend. Initially, the motion will be irregular, but after some time a pattern will appear. It usually resembles a honeycomb, though it can also be a series of parallel rolls. The same effect, called Bénard convection after the person who first described it, can also be seen in 'stone nests', regular arrays of stones which have been put in position by Bénard convection in the air, and in the motion of large numbers of a microorganism, *Euglena viridis*. The famous red spot on Jupiter is not a fixed coloured region on the surface of the planet, but another example of self-organisation. So is the complicated shape that can be formed by a simple drop of milk (Figure 2).

In most cases, it is not easy to see how self-organisation arises without working through a nonlinear mathematical model, which is largely why so few have been analysed until recently. One that can be seen intuitively, and which is also very important, is Jim Lovelock's model for the regulation of the Earth's temperature.[7]

Figure 2. Drop hitting the surface of milk

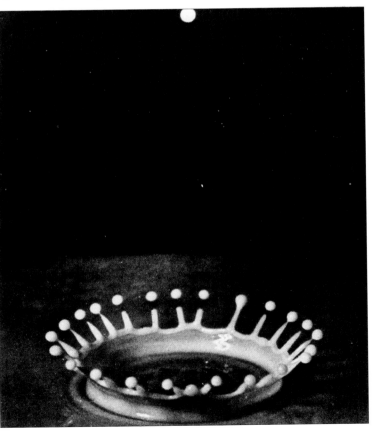

The Gaia hypothesis

When Lovelock put forward his 'Gaia hypothesis' that the Earth is self-regulating, he was immediately criticised by biologists. Applying the linear intuition I referred to before, they argued that since regulation is a coordinated phenomenon which serves a useful purpose, its cause must also be coordinated and purposeful. In other words, a regulated system must have been designed as such, either by an engineer or natural selection, or, if you prefer, the Creator.

Lovelock responded by showing how regulation could arise without design in a system which is a simplified model of the Earth.[8] He imagined a hypothetical planet called Daisyworld, in orbit around a star which, like our own sun, is very slowly becoming brighter. In the simplest version, the only form of life are daisies with black flowers. They grow best at 22.5C, less well above or below it, and not at all below 5 or above 40, though the seeds can survive.

If the sun is not bright enough, no daisies can grow, but when the planet reaches 5C, a few daisies appear. Since they are black, they make the planet darker, so it absorbs more light, which makes it warmer. This makes the daisies grow faster, which makes the planet darker, and so on. This positive feedback doesn't go on forever, partly because the daisies run out of space, and partly because if they raise the temperature to over 22.5C any more growth makes things worse for themselves, not better. On the other hand, if the solar luminosity continues to increase (or even if it decreases) the temperature remains almost unchanged.

The regulation is even more effective if there are white daisies as well, though this is harder to see without the equations. When both kinds are present, each species generally does better than it would if it were alone. If we want to interpret a dynamic in anthropomorphic terms, in this system cooperation is more important than competition.

This model shows how regulation can arise without design. What is more, a more complicated version of the principle almost certainly applies to the real Earth, which has in fact maintained a remarkably constant temperature through geological time, even though the Sun is now about a third brighter than it used to be. The same principle may also explain how regulation has arisen in organisms as well, for example in the maintenance of constant level of blood glucose in humans and other mammals by a combination of simple positive and negative feedbacks.[9]

Generic properties

A characteristic feature of nonlinear systems is that they often have generic properties, i.e. properties which occur time and time again in different systems and in different contexts. We do not fully understand why this is so, though some progress has been made, but at least we can see why it should be a consequence of nonlinearity. Linear systems are shaped by the forces that act on them, and so they will have the same form only if the forces were similar. Nonlinear systems are more autonomous, which makes it possible that they will have generic properties, though it does not explain how they arise.

1. Catastrophe theory

The best understood example is catastrophe theory, developed by the French mathematician René Thom about 40 years ago.[10] He showed that if boundaries between regions are formed by processes that can be described by any one of a very large class of differential equations, then they must have one of a very small number of shapes. The cusped shape of a supersonic shock wave is not an artefact of the way it is formed: it is about the only shape it could have.

This does not, however, mean that the problem is solved. The major limitation is that catastrophe theory is only local, i.e. it tells us what can happen around one focus of activity. That is sufficient to explain a sonic boom, because while it extends over a large region it is all centred on one point, the position of the aircraft. But it is too limited for biology, which was the subject Thom was most interested in and in which the problem of form is the most important, and no one has so far managed to extend the theory in the way that would be needed.

Some progress has, however, been made. For example, Alan Turing[11] showed how a simple nonlinear process, involving an interaction between reaction and diffusion, could produce patterns in an originally uniform region of tissue. This was a very important result, because by demonstrating that patterns can arise *de novo*, i.e. without prepatterns, it enables us to avoid the danger of an infinite regress.

Unfortunately, few examples are known of patterns that actually are produced in this way, and it now seems clear that it is not a major mechanism of pattern formation in nature. Later workers, however, have been finding other, more plausible mechanisms, which operate on the same mathematical principle, even though the equations that describe them can be quite different. They have also found that the patterns that are produced have many features in common with those predicted by the Turing mechanism, for example that the number of 'repeats' depends on the length of the region and that two dimensional patterns tend to be very irregular unless they are built up one dimension at a time.

2. Phyllotaxis

On many plants, the leaves are arranged along a spiral up the stem, with each leaf at an angle of (on average) 137.5° from the one before. This has been known for a long time, and has fascinated scientists because 137.5 is a golden section of 360. If you choose a leaf at random and then start numbering the leaves above it on the spiral, its two nearest neighbours will have numbers that are members of the Fibonacci sequence 1,1,2,3,5,8,13, . . . (each number is the sum of the two before it). The same is true for the florets on many flowers: in the case of sunflowers the numbers are often 55 and 89. It is easy to show that these two properties are related, but no one has found a convincing explanation of why they occur.

Recently, two French physicists, Douady and Couder,[12] carried out an experiment in which they allowed drops of a magnetised fluid to fall on to a plate at regular intervals. They found that as they made the interval shorter and shorter, the angle between successive drops became almost exactly $137.5°$.

Because physics is simpler than biology, Douady and Couder were able to write down the equations of motion and solve them. This allowed them to explain their own results, but not why the same angle occurs in plants, since that has nothing to do with magnetic dipoles.

They realised, however, that while the real mechanism – whatever it is – is different, it might lead to the same equations. To test this idea, they repeated the calculations, but using a different formula for the mutual repulsion between the drops. This naturally changed the equations of motion, but while the solutions were different for drops at longer intervals, as the intervals because shorter, the angle between successive drops still tended to the value $137.5°$. This angle, and the golden section and the Fibonacci numbers that go with it, are thus generic properties.

Genericity gives certain features a special status, like the archetypes of the pre-Darwinian biologists like Goethe and Geoffroy Saint Hilaire. They are the natural building blocks of a wide variety of phenomena. We can therefore use them without having to justify in detail why they should appear in a particular context.

In science we are used to arguments that begin like this: 'we know, or at least suppose, that the mechanism for this process is such and such, and from that we can compute that there will be a cusp. Knowing that there is a cusp, we can now predict . . .'

Naturally, we would still prefer to do that if we can. But if we cannot, which is likely to be case when we are studying complex phenomena, we can begin instead: 'we do not know the mechanism, but whatever it is, in these circumstances it is likely to produce a cusp. Assuming that there is a cusp, we can now predict . . .' This is not as certain as before, to be sure, but it is a way of making progress when the traditional method fails because of the complexity – which in some subjects is likely to be almost all the time.

Conclusions

In recent years, mathematicians have derived many interesting and important results concerning nonlinear systems. They have also become adept at applying the techniques of nonlinearity to conventional problems. Less has been accomplished towards exploring new ways of applying mathematics, especially those to do with genericity. The controversy that surrounded catastrophe theory in the late 1970s (the effects of which can be felt even today) arose because neither the proponents nor the critics were accustomed to the new sort of modelling. The arguments were similar to the debates about structuralism in some other fields, and of course this is not a coincidence: there are elements of structuralism in the new approach.

The Newtonian paradigm places the emphasis on external forces: gravity, natural selection, the market, and so on. Taking nonlinearity into effect means we concentrate more on the system: in evolution the developmental system of the organism, in economics the nature of society and the people who make it up. It does not, as do relativity and quantum mechanics, introduce entirely new scientific principles, but it can completely alter the direction of our research all the same.

Nonlinearity puts more responsibility on the individual. Chaos ensures that the future is not predetermined, and nonlinearity tells us that we cannot put all the blame for what happens on the outside world. The fault, dear Brutus, lies not in our stars but in ourselves . . .

Department of Mathematics, King's College, Strand, London WC2R 2LS.

Notes

1 See for example, E O Wilson, *Sociobiology, the New Synthesis*, Harvard University Press (Cambridge) 1975.

2 See Mae-Wan Ho's article in this issue; also her book *The Rainbow and the Worm*, World Scientific (Singapore), 1993.

3 E N Lorenz, 'Deterministic nonperiodic flow', *Journal of Atmospheric Science* 20, 1963, pp130-141.

4 C H Waddington, *The Strategy of the Genes*. George Allen and Unwin (London), 1957.

5 P T Saunders, 'The organism as a dynamical system', in *Thinking About Biology* (Santa Fe Institute Studies in the Sciences of Complexity, Vol III) W Stein and F J Varela (eds), Addison Wesley (Reading), 1993.

6 N Eldredge and S J Gould, 'Punctuated Equilibria: an Alternative to Phyletic Gradualism', in T J M Schopf (ed), *Models in Paleobiology*, Freeman Cooper (San Francisco), 1972, pp82-115.

7 J E Lovelock, *Gaia, a New Look at Life on Earth*, Oxford University Press (Oxford), 1979; *The Ages of Gaia*, Oxford University Press (Oxford), 1988.

8 A J Watson and J E Lovelock, 'Biological homeostasis of the global environment: the parable of Daisyworld', *Tellus* 35B, pp284-89. See also P T Saunders, 'Evolution without natural selection: further implications of the Daisyworld parable', *Journal of Theoretical Biology* 166 , 1994, pp365-73.

9 J H Koeslag, P T Saunders and J A Wessels, 'Glucose homeostasis with infinite gain: An application of the Daisyworld parable?' *Journal of Endocrinology*, 1997 (in press).

10 R Thom, *Stabilité Struturelle et Morphogénèse*, W A Benjamin, Reading, 1972. (English translation by D H Fowler, *Structural Stability and Morphogenesis*, W A Benjamin, Reading, 1975.) For a much simpler introduction, see P T Saunders, *An Introduction to Catastrophe Theory*, Cambridge University Press (Cambridge), 1980.

11 A Turing, 'The chemical basis of morphogenesis', *Transactions of the Royal Society of London* B641, 1952, pp37-72.

12 S Douady and Y Couder, 'Phyllotaxis as a physical self-organized growth process', *Physical Review Letters* 68, 1992, pp2098-2101.

DANIEL LIBESKIND
BETWEEN THE LINES
Berlin

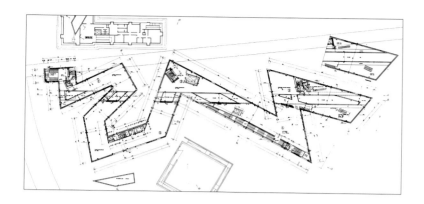

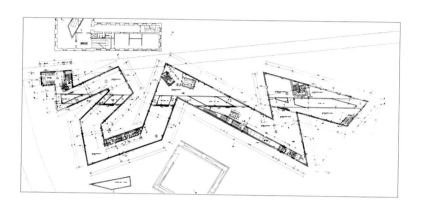

The official name of the project is the 'Extension of the Berlin Museum with the Jewish Museum Department' but I have called it 'Between the Lines'. I call it this because it is a project about two lines of thinking, organisation and relationship. One is a straight line, but broken into many fragments; the other is a tortuous line, but continuing infinitely. These two lines develop architecturally and pro-grammatically through a limited but definite dialogue. They also fall apart, become disengaged, and are seen as separated. In this way, they expose a void that runs through this museum and through Architecture – a discontinuous void.

The site is the centre of the old city of Berlin on Lindenstrasse, near the famous Baroque intersection of Wilhelmstrasse, Friedrichstrasse and Lindenstrasse. At the same time, I felt that the *physical* trace of Berlin was not the only trace but rather that there was an invisible matrix or anam-nesis of connections in relationship. I found this connection between figures of Germans and Jews; between the particu-lar history of Berlin, and between the Jewish history of Germany and of Berlin.

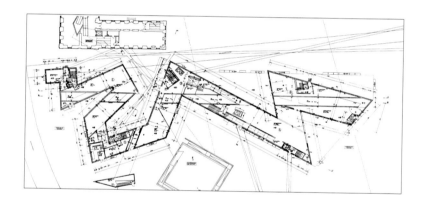

I felt that certain people and particularly certain writers, scientists, composers, artists and poets formed the link between Jewish tradition and German culture. So I found this connection and I plotted an irrational matrix which was in the form of a system of squared triangles which would yield some reference to the emble-matics of a compressed and distorted star: the yellow star that was so frequently worn on this very site.

I looked for addresses of where these people lived or where they worked. For example, someone like Rachel Varnhagen I connected to Friedrich Schleiermacher, and Paul Celan to someone like Mies van der Rohe and so on, and I was quite surprised that it was not so difficult to sense and plot the addresses of these people; that they formed a particular urban and cultural constellation of Universal History. This is one aspect of the project.

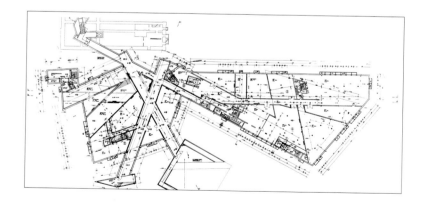

FROM ABOVE: Second floor plan; first floor plan; ground floor plan; basement plan; OPPOSITE: View of Holocaust void

OPPOSITE: View up main stair;
ABOVE: Finished facade
RIGHT: Aerial view

Another aspect was Arnold Schoenberg. I was always interested in the music of Schoenberg and in particular his period in Berlin. His greatest work is an opera called *Moses and Aaron*. For some reason the logic of the text, which was the relationship between Moses and Aaron – between, one can say, the revealed and unimaginable truth and the spoken and mass-produced people's truth – led to an impasse in which the music, the text written by Schoenberg, could not be completed. In the end, Moses doesn't sing, he just speaks, 'oh word, thou word': a form of communication which is opposed to the norm of opera wherein performance usually obliterates the text. When there is singing the words can not be understood but when it has ceased one understands very well the missing word uttered by Moses, which is the call for the deed. This was the second aspect of the project.

The third aspect was my interest in the names of those people who were deported from Berlin during the fatal years of the Holocaust, that one knows only historically. I received from Bonn two very large volumes called *Gedenkbuch*, which make a strong impression because all they contain are names; just names, dates of birth, dates of deportation and presumed places where these people were murdered. So I looked for the names of all the Berliners and where they had died – in Riga, in Lodz, in all the concentration camps.

The fourth aspect of the project, which is formed by Walter Benjamin's *One Way Street*, is incorporated into the continuous sequence of 60 sections along the zig-zag, each of which represents one of the 'Stations of the Star' described in his text.

To summarise this four-fold structure: the first aspect is the invisible and irrationally connected star which shines with absent light of individual address; the second one is the cut of Act II of *Moses and Aaron* which has to do with the non-musical fulfilment of the word; the third aspect is that of the deported or missing Berliners, and the fourth aspect is Walter Benjamin's urban apocalypse along the One Way Street.

In specific terms it is a very large building: more than 10,000 square metres. Its budget is something like 120 million Deutschmarks. The building goes under the existing building, crisscrosses underground and materialises itself independently on the outside. The existing building is tied to the extension underground, preserving the contradictory autonomy of both the old building and the new building on the surface, while binding the two together in depth, underground.

Out of the terminus of history, which is nothing other than the Holocaust with its concentrated space of annihilation and complete burn-out of meaningful development of the city, and of humanity – out of this event which shatters this place comes that which cannot really be related by architecture. The past fatality of the German-Jewish cultural relation in Berlin is enacted now in the realm of the invisible. (It is this remoteness which I have tried to bring to consciousness.)

The work is conceived as a museum for all Berliners, for all citizens. Not only those of the present, but those of the future and the past who should find their heritage and hope in this particular place, which is to transcend involvement and become participation. With its special emphasis on housing the Jewish Museum, it is an attempt to give a voice to a common fate – to the contradictions of the ordered and disordered, the chosen and not chosen, the vocal and silent.

Thus the new extension is conceived as an emblem, where the invisible – the void – makes itself apparent as such. The void and the invisible are the structural features that have been gathered in the space of Berlin and exposed in an architecture in which the unnamed remains in the names which keep still.

In terms of the city, the idea is to give a new value to the existing context, the historical context, by transforming the urban field into an open and what I would call a hope-oriented matrix. The proposed expansion, therefore, is characterised by a series of real and implied transformations of the site. The compactness of traditional street patterns is gradually

dissolved from Baroque origins and then related diagonally across to the 1960s housing development and the new IBA projects.

In other words, to put it simply, the museum is a zig-zag with a structural rib which is the void of the Jewish Museum running across it. And this void is something which every participant in the museum will experience as his or her absent presence.

That is basically a summary of how the building works. It is not a collage or a collision or simply a dialectic, but a new type of organisation which is organised around a centre which is not: the void around what is not visible. And what is not visible is the collection of this Jewish Museum, which is reducible to archival and archeological material since its physicality has disappeared.

The problem of the Jewish Museum in Berlin is taken as the problem of culture itself. Let us put it this way as the problem of an avant-garde humanity; an avant-garde that has been incinerated in its own history, in the Holocaust. In this sense, I believe this scheme joins architecture to questions that are now relevant to all humanity. What I have tried to convey is that the Jewish history of Berlin is not separable from the history of Modernity, from the destiny of this incineration of history: they are bound together. However, they are bound not through any obvious forms but rather through a negativity; through an absence of meaning of history and an absence of artefacts.

Absence, therefore serves as a way of binding in depth, and in a totally different manner, the shared hopes of people. It is a conception which is absolutely opposed to reducing the museum or architecture to a detached memorial or to a memorable detachment. A conception, rather, which reintegrates Jewish Berlin History through the unhealable wound of faith, which in the words of Thomas Aquinas is the 'substance of things hoped for; proof of things invisible'.

Transcript of a talk given at Hannover University, 5th December, 1989

OPPOSITE: Detail of facade

DANIEL LIBESKIND

THE VICTORIA & ALBERT MUSEUM BOILERHOUSE EXTENSION
London

Model perspectives

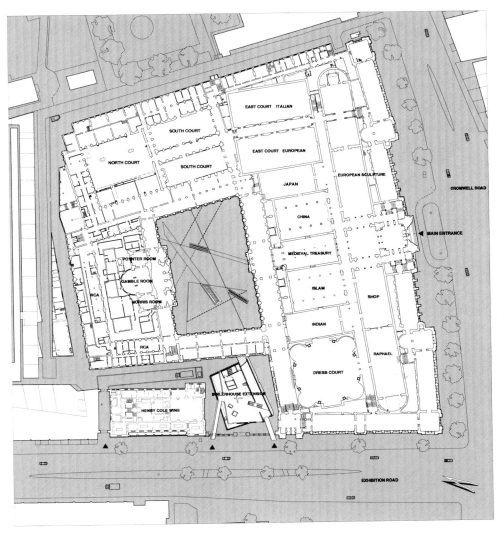

Location plan

When facing the old entrance of the Victoria & Albert Museum, one is confronted by two words to the left and right of the main gate: *Imagination* and *Knowledge*. This twin inscription describes the inspirational force, or muse, steering the idea of the museum. In the next century, this profound dialectic must continue to engage the wide public and open the experience of the visitor to new ways of viewing and using the museum. The museum of the 21st century must itself be open to the future of still unknown possibilities lodged between these guideposts.

The Victoria & Albert Museum has taken up this challenge with a proposal to build an extension including an integrated mixture of exhibition spaces, educational facilities and accommodation for new methods of interactive orientation. The V&A's mission to provide a gateway to the 21st century via its own rich and diverse collection requires a vision that gives new significance to its great traditions and goes beyond the purely passive relation between the arts and the public. This proposal offers new kinds of experience eluding the closure that would categorise the museum as 'ready-made', rigidly defined, or passively neutral.

The design (1996-99) is structured around three dimensions: the spiral movement of art and history; the interlocking of inside and outside, and the labyrinth of discovery. It takes these dimensions and translates them into a coherent ensemble of functionally related spaces.

The spiral of art and history manifests itself in the overall form of the extension building and its circulation system. The enclosure is created out of a continuous wall, whose extent mirrors that of the perimeter walls of the entire V&A block, spiralling around a virtual and ever shifting vertical axis. Visitors are implicated in a spiral movement as they circulate through the various functions of the museum. This movement distributes the public in a dynamic way to the rest of the museum through strategic connections

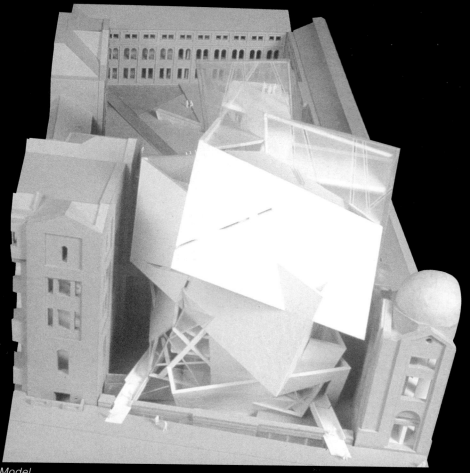

Model

and is a counterpoint to the lateral, horizontal movement in the existing buildings.

Interlocking of the inside and the outside of the new building is created by the winding and the unwinding spiral which brings the visitor into close relation with history and the present, the city and the museum, through a direct experience of interpenetrating views and histories. From the extension one sees ever-changing views of the existing facades and the skyline of London, while from within the old museum block, one is reoriented by the shifting movement of the new building.

The relationship between form and function generates a variety of sequential and dramatic narratives of space and light. The whole is a composition of layered sequences in which the new building becomes a veritable beacon of energy towards the inside and outside world.

The labyrinth of discovery is the organisational leitmotiv mediating between the existing galleries and the museum's new programme requirements. The image of the labyrinth is not only a symbolic device but a reinforcement and intensification of the unique qualities of the V&A. This emblem of a heterogeneous and open system of organisation for the artefacts and exhibitions provides a diversity of experiences woven into a net of similarities and differences – an aggregate of traces about unexpected topoi still to be explored. The seamless transition from place to place, and floor to floor envelops the visitor in a unique continuity throughout the many dimensions of the Museum as a whole.

The spiral form fuses the archaic and the new in its organisation and urban image. It provides an emblem articulating the cross-cultural collections of the V&A, the multi-cultural profile of its visitors and the fusion of the arts, technology and

history. The structure of discovery in the new extension is a microcosm of the multi-faceted order of the museum and a gateway to the history of the decorative arts. The visitors are celebrated as participants in the sensory and intellectual experience, an ongoing discovery of the drama of art and its history.

The structure and cladding of the new extension are formed by the 'fractile', a new kind of tile pattern whose economy allows a multiform language to emerge out of an elementary geometric piece, interpreted in a variety of different ways. As a strategy towards the surface, the 'fractile' bridges the gap between the wondrous tiles of Granada and Isfahan and the tile technology used on the space shuttle, bringing the decorative arts onto the surface of the building. This pattern offers endless variation in formal articulation and the relationship between surface and structure within the economy of building construction. The design of motifs and patterns could be developed through the educational activities of the museum via an interactive participation programme, so that the building surface becomes an ongoing expression of unpredictable yet controlled interactions between Arts and Crafts, around the theme of the contemporary museum.

The new extension is divided into two parts:

• In the upper levels, an interactive field continuum of traditional and non-Cartesian spaces is enclosed within the folds of the spiral. These floors house the new galleries for the permanent collections, the orientation centre and the museum administration on several upper floors. The exhibition galleries are lifted out of the anonymity with which such spaces are often associated, and instead articulate a new configuration responding to the creative tension between spatial relation and programmatic field. Out of these special qualities, spaces are created which can accommodate a wide variety of exhibitions, from traditional installations to new events emerging out of technological media forms. In this way, the kinetic and sensory experience offers multiple ways of discovering the familiar.

• In the levels below the street, one finds a highly modern gallery for temporary exhibitions, educational facilities and an auditorium for performances, theatre, lectures and film. These diverse activities are organised within a rigorous functional system designed for maximum flexibility. These spaces extend under the existing buildings into the Pirelli gardens, tying the extension in depth to the heart of the museum complex and functioning as the foundation for the galleries above – the infrastructure supporting the lantern of history.

These two parts are separated by the entrance lobby spaces, which the visitor enters across a bridge overlooking a new sunken garden out of which the building grows. In this way an open and inviting new entrance is created as an exhilarating symbol of the dynamics of the museum's diverse exhibitions. Fronting and visible from the street is a gift shop and bookstore, welcoming the visitor into the museum lobby. Once inside, one sees the central position of the information and ticket desk and the core of elevators.

The lobby space extends vertically down to the restaurant and children's play area directly below which look out over the new garden. These two levels form a unit constituting the lobby space as a whole, connected at ground level to the existing buildings.

From the lobby, visitors to the museum's collections take the glazed express elevator directly to the observatory of the orientation centre on the top floor; glimpsing along the way the offerings in the new permanent collection galleries. From here, overlooking the Pirelli Garden and the roofscape of the entire museum, a route around the galleries can be planned using the materials and technologies of the centre. Next to this is a café/bar looking over the museum and the city. The route from here to the museum proper takes the visitor on a spiral descent via escalators to the new galleries housing the permanent collection and back towards the lobby. Linkages to the rest of the museum's collections are located on various levels along this route, allowing direct connection from multiple points.

Visitors to the museum who wish to see the temporary exhibition, or use the educational facilities, access these spaces by descending directly from the lobby; passing on their way the restaurant and children's play area. The auditorium is directly underneath this, on the same level as the temporary exhibition galleries which extend under the Pirelli Garden. From this point, a staircase leads straight to the educational facilities and workshops beneath and a ramp rises into the garden creating a connection between the changing exhibitions, the learning facilities and the rest of the museum. The garden itself is restructured as a dynamic landscape punctuated by skylights which provide the temporary exhibition galleries and educational spaces with natural light.

From Exhibition Road a second bridge offers alternative access to the lobby and direct entrance for groups to the temporary exhibitions, auditorium and educational facilities. By lowering the Webb Screen to face the garden, it becomes the frame for an outdoor exhibition space, visible from the lower levels of the new extension. In this way Aston Webb's architecture is given new significance; no longer a screen but a frame for activity and a stage for events.

The administration spaces of the programme are located on several floors at the top of the spiral near the orientation centre, with separate access via a bridge link to the Henry Cole Wing. The offices are provided with views of the existing museum buildings and are connected to the new exhibition spaces by an atrium. Although embedded within the exhibition galleries they can thus function completely independently of the public parts of the extension.

The new museum for the V&A, constructed on its last available site (1998-2001), is perhaps best likened to the last chord of a symphony. Only when this chord is played do the first notes acquire the form of their fulfilment. This proposal extends the zone of boundaries and connections (between old/new; inside/outside; structure/form; architecture/decoration; technology/craft) by shifting them to ever new and open perspectives, intersections and relations through its fugal construction. By opening instead of closing the block of the V&A, this last chord does not end the music of the museum, but extends it towards unknown and future horizons of the mind and of space.

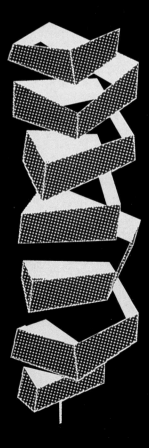

Engineering design diagram of wall

FOREIGN OFFICE ARCHITECTS
YOKOHAMA INTERNATIONAL PORT TERMINAL
Yokohama, Japan

The concept of *ni-wa-minato*, proposed by the client as the starting point of the project, suggests a mediation between garden and harbour, but also between the citizens of Yokohama and those from the outside world. This proposal for the new Yokohama terminal aims for an artefactual rather than a representational mediation between the two elements of this concept.

The artefact will operate as a mediating device between the two large social machines that make up the new institution: the system of public spaces of Yokohama and the management of cruise passenger flow. The components are used as a device for reciprocal *deterritorialisation*: a public space that wraps around the terminal, neglecting its symbolic presence as a gate, decodifying the rituals of travel, and a functional structure which becomes the mould of an a-typological public space, a landscape with no instructions for occupation. The aim is to achieve a mediation of a differential nature: a machine of integration that allows us to move imperceptibly through different states, turning states into degrees of intensity, countering the effects of rigid segmentation usually produced by social mechanisms, especially those dedicated to maintaining borders. The proposed artefact will reduce the amount of energy required to pass between the states, articulating in a differential mode the various segments of the programme throughout a continuously varied form: from local citizens to foreign visitor, from *flâneur* to business traveller, from voyeur to exhibitionist, from performer to spectator.

Using the ground surface to create a complementary public space to Yamashita Park, the proposal will result in the first perpendicular penetration of the urban space within the Yokohama Bay. The ground of the city will be seamlessly connected to the boarding level and from there it will bifurcate to produce a multiplicity of urban events. As a consequence, the building will become an extension of the city.

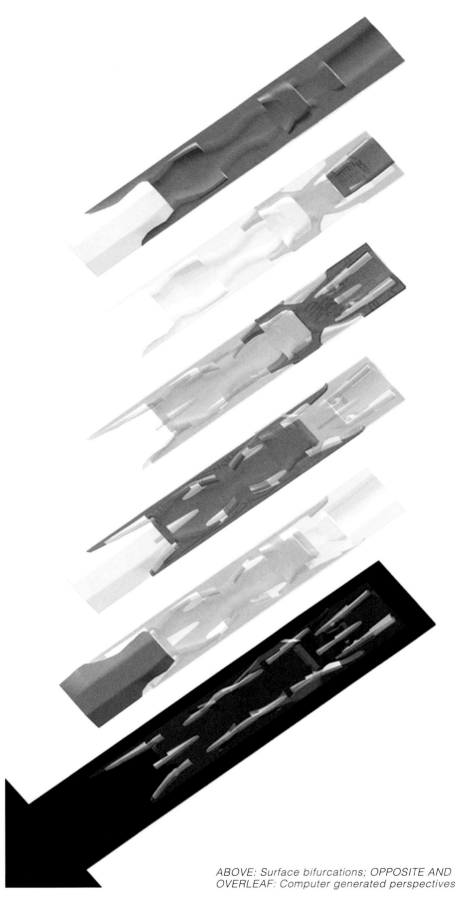

ABOVE: Surface bifurcations; OPPOSITE AND OVERLEAF: Computer generated perspectives

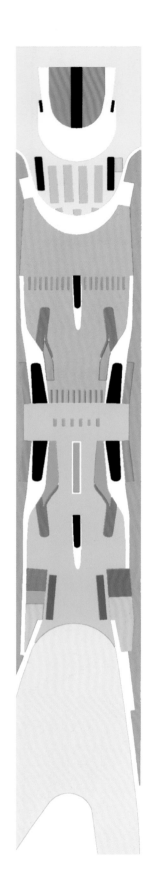

Solenoid

The plaza/terminal's function will not be simply to organise flows, but also to construct a field of urban intensity through enhancement of multiple paths and directions. In the Osanbashi plaza, the aim is to produce a *solenoid* – an inductive organisation of flows – to project urban intensity within the bay.

Battlefield

Owing to the varying size and schedules of the carriers, there will be constant fluctuations in the volume of space required by the domestic and international facilities. This calls for a structure in which the boundaries between domestic and international could be shifted to allow for such fluctuations. However, the demand for flexibility did not lead us to create a space of the utmost neutrality, but led to a highly differentiated structure, a seamless milieu which allows for the broadest variety of scenarios: an ideal battlefield where the strategic position of a small number of elements will substantially affect the definition of the frontier. Mobile or collapsible physical barriers and surveillance points will enable the reconfiguration of the borders between territories, allowing the terminal to be occupied by locals or invaded by foreigners.

Origami

The surface of the ground folds on to itself, forming creases that not only produce and contain paths through the building, creating the differential conditions for the programme, but also provide structural strength. Thus the traditional separation between building-envelope and load-bearing structure disappears.

The use of segmented elements such as columns, walls or floors has been avoided in favour of a move towards a materiality where the differentiation of structural stresses is not determined by coded elements but by singularities within a material continuum.

Mille-Feuille

An entirely steel construction is proposed in order to provide the flexibility and lightness which are needed to resist earthquake damage. The construction system extends the concept of accumulating layers – structural layers, programmatic layers, finishes, etc.

No return

The building's circulation system has been organised as a series of loops in which the borders between the dynamic and the static have been removed. A variety of alternative paths will intensify the experience of passing through the building by duplicating the number of events which are encountered.

Weaving

The circulation system used by the citizens of Yokohama and the boat passengers is interwoven by reinforcing the connections between them. Interaction between the two systems is further increased by the inversion of the conventional position of the terminal facilities and the leisure facilities.

OPPOSITE: Plans; ABOVE: Model sections; BELOW: Longitudinal section

THE FRACTAL CITY

MICHAEL BATTY AND PAUL LONGLEY

Abstract

A new science of form based on fractal geometry has emerged during the last 10 years. Fractals, or fractal objects as they are called, are irregular in shape but their irregularity is similar across many scales, thus enabling them to be described mathematically, and to be generated computationally. Fractals cannot be described using the geometry of regular figures based on points, lines, planes – the geometry of Euclid – for they exist between dimensions and therefore must be measured by means of their fractional or fractal dimension. Good examples are natural features and systems such as coastlines, mountainous terrain, and trees, but man-made artefacts such as silicon chips, stock market behaviour and even social organisations are fractals. Here we show that the morphology of cities is fractal. Their study using fractal geometry enables rich, predictive models of their structure to be developed, yielding new insights into how cities develop and how ideal cities can be formed.

The new science of cities

In the mid-20th century, those thinking about cities believed that they were clearly organised, simply ordered, and thus predictable, capable of being designed and planned in such a way that the quality of life of their residents could be directly improved by manipulating their physical form. This was a view that was widely held throughout architecture, indeed throughout the social sciences. It was founded on the belief that the social world, and its representation in physical artefacts such as cities was coherent and understandable in the same way that the physical world had been understood since the Enlightenment. The evident success of physics in providing an intellectual foundation for material technologies and the triumph of rationality through the application of the scientific method could be transferred wholesale and emulated in the social world, it was argued. Conscious and deliberate attempts at social engineering, as in the kind of architecture and urban planning which has dominated Western societies for the last 50 years and now the developing world, was the result.

As we approach the millennium, all this seems naive. The rational scientific programme has been split asunder in the last 20 years. Our understanding of systems in the small does not add up in any measure to our understanding in the large. Our theories and methods do not scale. The whole is more than the sum of the parts and physics as a basis for everything has been widely discredited. The limits imposed by theories of incompleteness, uncertainty, and complexity have destroyed any hope of a complete understanding and although there are some who still believe that physics will yet produce deeper theory, there is little hope that this will provide anything other than a mathematical tidying up of ever more tortuous logic. Dreams of a final theory are a chimera. Systems everywhere are simply too complex to be reduced to the tenets of conventional science. In the social world, prediction is logically impossible – although magic in the form of unpredictable new technologies is not! – while attempts at social engineering in the blunt manner of the mid-century have made the human condition worse rather than better.

Cities, the way we understand them, and the way we plan them demonstrate all the features of this crisis of rationality. Attempts at building mathematical models of their structure which began more than a generation ago were unable to yield realistic predictions even in the narrowest terms. They proved incapable of dealing with any kind of future which embodied creative development, surprise or novelty, now largely regarded as the seeds of social change. The massive explosions of population and their subsequent taming, and the emergence of world or global cities were not anticipated. Likewise, the impact of information and communication technologies and the rise of the network city could not be predicted, while at more local scales the development of edge cities, the refocusing of the city on suburbia, and the collapse of public transport systems inside Western cities have only been explicable in hindsight. In short, conventional science was unable to predict or even sense the emergence of new kinds of cities, new urban forms. In parallel, the repercussions of the disastrous experiments in social housing, of detailed planning controls on stifling economic development, and of transport systems which generated ever greater pollution and congestion, were nowhere anticipated. It is little surprise that the public and the polity, even the planners themselves, turned against the ideologies which produced such abhorrent results in our cities in the name of efficiency and equity.

The general response to these dilemmas has been the retreat into post-modernism. New urban theory is based on understanding cities in terms of their superficial structure through the kaleidoscope of social and physical complexity that clearly marks the intractability and ambiguity of the late 20th-century city. The search for order in cities in traditional scientific terms which associates cause to effect has all but been abandoned by the avant-garde. But amidst the ruins of this old science, a new science is emerging. Over the last 20 years, the view has been gaining ground that *insight* not *prediction* must be the goal of science. This has been spurred on by discoveries in mathematics in the late 1960s that superficially simple, deterministic systems from which equally simple and incontestable predictions have always been assumed, were not predictable in the traditional sense. The fact that simple systems were manifested with a level of complexity that was completely unknown, went some way to explain why more complex systems, which were often built from such simpler elements, were entirely unpredictable, in fact even chaotic. Cities, the weather, stock markets, are all examples which demonstrate chaotic behaviour under certain regimes, whose traditional models were unable to yield predictions with scale and form known in advance. In mathematical terms, this is largely due to the fact that the mathematical space within which such models operate is so convoluted and infinitely divisible that it is impossible to guess the accurate starting position of the systems within this space. In fact, it is impossible to know the position of the system and therefore impossible to make any form of prediction in the kind of precise terms that Newtonian science demands and assumes.

Such systems (and it can be shown that many, in fact most real systems can be so characterised) are thus largely unknowable. Even if their initial conditions and positions could be known, slight perturbations – random effects – would push their evolution into uncharted territory. Predicting weather is the classic example of such chaos. Edward Lorenz, who originally discovered chaos, presented a famous paper in 1972 entitled: 'Does the Flap of a Butterfly's Wings in Brazil Set Off a Tornado in Texas?'. In short, simple and small effects are magnified quickly into large-scale effects due to the action of positive feedback whose effects build spontaneously and cumulatively on each other. Chaotic systems are thus very different from those that science has worked with for the last 200 years. We traditionally assumed that most systems were linear. When they change, they change gradually, in proportion to what is there already, and thus their future behaviour is predictable, knowable. In fact, many systems are not like this for they show discontinuities in their behaviour, marked by catastrophes and bifurcations; weather, the stock market, prison riots and in our own case, the emergence of edge cities and out-of-town centres, are all examples of systems which cannot be understood and predicted by the traditional methods of science. Systems which shoot off into new domains and realms, which bifurcate, characterise those where surprise, novelty, and creative effort are central, where qualitatively different kinds of outcomes occur which cannot be predicted by methods which assume that the future is a simple linear function of the past. In fact, when science is scaled up to the real world, when we work with real systems like the weather, the physics of the small scale and the laboratory no longer applies and everything we deal with shows signs of chaos. Chaotic systems are the rule, not the exception which is what has been discovered slowly and painfully in science during the last 20 years.

There are many aspects of this new science which can be used to generate insights into the growth and structure of cities but here we will focus on how this helps us to understand their physical form, their morphology. One of the reasons why chaos lay undiscovered for so long in science and mathematics was that the mathematical space in which chaotic systems exist is irregular in a way that defied conventional geometries. The same kinds of irregularity are widespread in the non-mathematical, in the material world, in the morphology of cities, in geomorphology, in ecology, in biology, and in social organisation. Features such as boundaries, the way forms are packed into each other and

into space, the way terrain is structured and the way objects vary across scale, can all be seen in terms of a new geometry of form which has intrinsic connections with the new science of complexity. We will explain this geometry herein.

Fractals: the new architecture of urban form

Mid-century, our understanding of cities was largely based on responses to their physical form. Urban problems and their solutions were predicated in physical terms but as the quest for a deeper understanding began, the link between physical form and socio-economic functioning was broken. Although urban patterns were suggestive of such functioning leading to analogies, for example, between the city and the human body, the city and the machine, a convincing theory of urban form in the manner proposed for biology by D'Arcy Thompson, was never forthcoming just as it never materialised in biology either. Consequently, physical form became abstracted to the point where socio-economic functioning was loaded on to highly simplistic spatial structures, with little direct relevance to the ways in which architects and planners continued to manipulate, transform, design, and plan the city. But a generation passed, the world changed, and slowly but surely, interest in physical form revived: a new approach emerged.

Let us begin by explaining this new approach to studying urban form which is rapidly becoming an essential cornerstone in the post-modern science of cities. Imagine an ideal city of Renaissance times with an elaborate fortified wall built in the shape of the snowflake shown in the sequence in Figure 1 overleaf. The reason for the shape of such fortifications was to maximise the length of the wall so that as many soldiers as possible could be packed into the town's defence. Let us make the assumption that to design a good wall, we can repeat the basic motif which elongates the wall at different scales, thus maximising its length from the basic triangle in Figure 1(a) to the snowflake in Figure 1(d). In this sequence of figures, we might think of the way the same shape or detail is added at each level as the way we see the outline of the town at different scales, 1(a) being the coarsest scale where we can only see the triangular outline, to the finest level, 1(d), where we have three levels of similarly-shaped detail superimposed on one another. In these figures, we have taken the wall on the north side of the town and reproduced its line between each shape, clearly showing how the town wall gets longer as the scale gets finer. The rule for Renaissance town design is: to get the longest wall possible, add the same kind of crenellation at each finer and finer scale until no more soldiers can be packed around the wall.

At the first scale, we can consider the basic length of wall as being 1 unit but divided into 3 subunits, each of 1/3 length – Figure 1(a). At the next scale down, we add another subunit of 1/3 length by taking the central subunit and forming a triangular displacement with two sides of 1/3, thus making the length of the

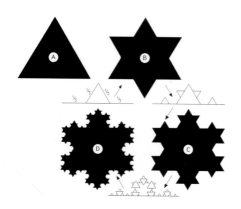

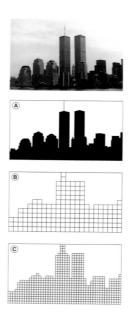

LEFT: *Figure 1*. *Generating the Koch Snowflake: a model of a fortified Renaissance town; RIGHT:* *Figure 2*. *The Manhattan skyline;* *Figure 3*. *The Manhattan skyline at two different scales*

new line 4/3. This is equivalent to taking the old line and introducing a kink in it to make it longer as we show between Figure 1(a) and 1(b). We can of course keep on doing this at each scale. At the next scale down, we take each subunit of 1/3 and introduce a triangular displacement of length 1/9, thus leading to each subunit increasing in length from 1/3 to 4/9, and the overall length of the line increasing from 4/3 to (4/3)*(4/3) = 16/9 as in Figure 1(c). At the next scale, doing the same leads to the length of the overall line increasing to (4/3)*(4/3)*(4/3) = 64/27, as in Figure 1(d). We could speculate that if we continue this process indefinitely, the length of the line increases without bound: its length is unlimited – infinite – with the length being $(4/3)^k$ where k is the index of the scale. Of course, the scale from which we see this snowflake is fixed at the scale of the page, but you might imagine this going on for ever, picking up more and more detail as the scale gets finer and finer, from earthscale to subatomic levels.

This poses a paradox: how can a line continue to increase in length when it is clear from the sequence in Figure 1 that the area which the line encloses is finite? In fact, the area of the snowflake will converge to a fixed value as more and more detail at smaller and smaller scales is added. This conundrum was first stated for a coastline in a famous paper called 'How Long is the Coast of Britain?' by Benoit Mandelbrot (1967), who launched the field of fractal geometry 30 years ago. When you view a coastline on a map, it is at a certain scale. As the scale gets finer, then more detail around the coast is picked up and its length increases. If you go down on to the beach, then you would have to make a decision as to whether you were to measure around every pebble, and definitional problems would loom. But in general as you descend to the microscopic level, the length of the line increases without bound and it is easy to show mathematically (as we have shown pictorially in Figure 1) that the answer to the Mandelbrot question is that the length of the coastline is infinite; or rather, not infinite, but undefined. In short, for objects like coastlines, length depends on scale and absolute geometric

measures are no longer relevant. These are the kind of objects which are fractals, and it is clear that every boundary in nature must be fractal.

This geometric paradox was known in the 19th century in mathematics and in geography. There is some evidence that Leonardo da Vinci reflected upon it and if Leonardo knew about it, there is a good chance that the Greeks knew about it too. The paradox is as old as the hills. What is new is that for the first time, we now understand it and we have a new geometry to deal with it. But there is much more to fractals than the problem of length. To progress, consider the snowflake in Figure 1 which is the clearest kind of example. We constructed this fractal and were able to calculate its length routinely by taking a simple motif – the triangle – which we reduced in scale, transforming its position so that the snowflake might be constructed at any scale. It is quite clear that the design is similar from scale to scale and that at finer scales, the fractal is constructed from scaled down versions of the larger scale. We say that the fractal is self-similar in that the whole is formed from scaled versions of its parts. Fractals, like this snowflake curve (sometimes called the Koch curve after its originator, Von Koch) are exactly self-similar but if a little bit of randomness is introduced, as in a coastline, the object might be statistically self-similar or self-affine. The point is that seemingly random and transformed shapes can repeat themselves across scale and are thus fractals in the formal sense.

Besides scale invariance shown through self-similarity, fractals have precise mathematical properties. Using the traditional geometry of Euclid, a point has dimension 0, a line dimension 1, a plane dimension 2, a volume dimension 3, and so on. Fractal lines lie between dimension 1 and 2. Look at the line in Figure 1. It is more than the straight line of dimension 1 but it fills less than the plane with dimension 2. It twists to fill some of the plane and intuitively we might think its dimension lies between 1 and 2. For the Koch curve, we can compute the dimension as 1.26 (or in exact terms (log 4)/(log 3)) but if we think of lines which are more irregular such as fjord coastlines or if we make the kink in the

snowflake more exaggerated, the fractal dimension rises. Lines that twist and turn all across the space have a fractal dimension nearer 2. In fact, if you were to colour a square with a pencil and impose the rule that you are not to take the pencil off the paper but colour the square with one continuous line, you generate something resembling a fractal with Euclidean dimension 1 – it is a line – but fractal dimension 2 – it is a space-filling curve.

Fractals can of course exist in any dimension. Groups of points that follow a line are fractal dusts which have a dimension between 0 and 1, terrain has a dimension greater than 2 but less than 3, and cross-sections through terrain generate fractal lines with dimension between 1 and 2. City skylines look like obvious candidates. In Figure 2, we show the Manhattan skyline and in Figure 3, we show how the simplified outline of the skyline – Figure 3(a) – can be represented at two scales, Figure 3(c) being half the scale of Figure 3(b). By counting the number of cells at these two scales and then normalising by scale, we use a method (called box-counting) to work out the fractal dimension of the Manhattan skyline which gives a value of 1.56. If we looked at the suburbs, which are all composed of one- and two-storey buildings and open space, the dimension is more likely to be around 1.1 or 1.2. Once you start looking for fractals, you will find them everywhere (which is the title of one of the basic mathematical books on the subject by Barnsley, *Fractals Everywhere* (1988). In fact, most natural and man-made objects are not composed of simple points, lines and planes but of irregularly scaled versions of these. Fractal geometry is clearly the geometry of nature which is in the title of Mandelbrot's classic work defining the field, *The Fractal Geometry of Nature* (1983), but is also the geometry of cities as we reflect in our book *Fractal Cities* (1994). It is time to look at how we can describe and model cities in these terms.

Fractals in nature and fractals in cities

Any form which is self-similar is likely to be fractal. If there is a regular motif or design which repeats itself as the structure grows or scales – through time or across space, then that structure can be envisaged as a hierarchy, and thus fractal organisation is hierarchical organisation. The very best example is a tree. A tree is clearly self-similar in that its branches usually split regularly as they contract (scale) with distance from the root or main trunk. Any part of the tree mirrors the whole tree from the roots to the twigs and even into the structure of its leaves. In fact a tree is the literal embodiment of a hierarchy in that if you turn it upside down, the resulting structure shows the order in which the branches and twigs are formed as the tree grows from its roots. Indeed, if you look at the roots, then these, too, have the same shape as the tree, with the same fractal growth reaching into the earth as well as the sky. A wonderful demonstration of a fractal is to break some twigs from a tree, and view these twigs by blurring one's eyes, imagining that the twigs are the whole tree: the effect can be startling, just as the same can be seen in rock scree that has been formed by erosion on a mountain slope – the entire mountain form is contained within the scree, the scree being a smaller version of the same: this is what fractals in nature are all about.

Trees can be measured in two dimensions as elevations, or as plans, as cross-sections in the plane, or as objects that fill the plane, all giving rise to different fractal dimensions in the same way that cities can be envisaged as maps, as building structures that fill the third dimension, or as boundaries, or cross-sections such as the Manhattan skyline. We show the self-similarity of a number of trees in Figure 4 where the idea of hierarchy is quite clear and where suitable rendering provides very realistic looking trees. Note also that in the Koch curve of Figure 1, if the displacement is made into a spike, the resultant shape resembles a tree-like form, the so called Koch forest. Wherever self-similarity is generated across scales by repetition of a simple branching, then tree-like structures emerge as we will see for cities in terms of road networks, in geomorphology in terms of river and other water channels, and in the human body in terms of nerves and blood flow. In Figure 5 we show what is perhaps the best example of a fractal model of nature developed to date. This is Barnsley's fern (1988), which has been generated using a special mathematical technique which takes a real fern, computes how its branches transform into one another at different scales and then literally throws random dots at the page in such a way that only those dots that reflect the mathematical structure stick. In this way you can generate ever more levels of detail in a fractal object from whatever scale, with ever more realistic rendering.

So far, we have illustrated idealised fractals and real fractals, and fractals which are generated using models which reflect reality. The snowflake is idealised, the Manhattan skyline real, Barnsley's fern a model of reality. These distinctions run throughout science, and certainly throughout our use of fractal geometry to design, .measure, and model cities. All our examples here reflect these distinctions and in the rest of this essay, we will show how different characterisations of urban form develop these different aspects of fractal geometry. Part of the challenge of this new science is to use this geometry creatively to measure, model and design; our book *Fractal Cities* contains many examples of this approach and we will now develop some of these here to illustrate their wide applicability.

Let us look at the way we might generate hypothetical fractal cities, starting with the assumption that cities of the past largely grew around their historic core. We plant a seed and then apply some local rule which embodies our shape motif, to the development already created. In Figure 6, we show four variations on this theme. The first, where we get rings of development, is the situation where everything is developed in the vicinity of each seed. No motif is applied and everything is developed with the shading showing the order in which the city grows around its core. The city fills its entire space and its fractal dimension is 2, the same as its Euclidean. As we make the motif more structured, sparser cities are grown which form the other three examples in this figure. In the top right-hand corner, the structure assumes that a cell is developed if there is one, and only one, already developed cell in the local neighbourhood. The bottom left-hand figure is the same with one or two developed cells in the neighbourhood. The bottom right-hand shape is created when the neighbourhood is restricted to cells north, south, east, and west of the cell in question with the rule that a cell is newly developed if only one cell in the neighbourhood is already developed. We can of course generate landscapes of these cities by planting many seeds and we show the kind of fractal carpet produced by applying the single cell rule in Figure 7. There are many other variants. In Figure 8 we show how we can grow a sparser structure – one which is called a Sierpinski gasket after the mathematician who discovered it – which spans the space and wraps around it. This is the kind of structure that we might envisage would be required when we colonise outer space – the kind envisaged by Arthur C Clarke in his recent book *3001: The Final Odyssey* where space cities require sparse, light structures which span space in more economical ways than the way we have built high density cities like London and New York.

There are three important points that need to be made about these hypothetical patterns. First, fractals do not only exist in space but also in time. The fractal carpets in Figures 6 to 8 illustrate how the motifs appear both spatially and temporally as the colour coding shows. Finding fractal patterns in time is harder than in space because the way we represent cities is usually in terms of space and we must disentangle space in terms of time to discover these. The second point relates to the

way we generate fractals. Clearly the procedures we use must be repetitive, iterative, or recursive as mathematicians call them. The way we constructed the snowflake in Figure 1 shows the basic idea of repeating and scaling the basic motif and placing it appropriately on the object as smaller and smaller versions of the overall pattern. Barnsley's (1988) iteration function system (IFS) is one such method but in Figures 6 to 8 we have defined the motifs in terms of cells or pixels on the computer screen and used a technique called cellular automata to generate these pictures. This way of modelling is basic to the new science of complexity which is being used widely to simulate space-time patterns, and it forms the essence of the creation of artificial life which represents the current synthesis of biology and computer science.

Thirdly, fractal geometry would be of no more than cursory interest if it were not for the profound idea that complex entities can only be understood in terms of very simple entities that comprise them. Cities display enormous variety but there is order to this variety and this order is clearly made up of very simple elements. Much of economic urban theory is premised on such order: for example, the distribution of places of different sizes and the way they grow is consistent with fractal theory, and although these theories have been under development for over one hundred years, they have been hard to tie to real city forms. Fractal geometry not only explains how order emerges from simple, local components but how complexity emerges. There is now real hope that appropriate ways of anticipating urban change, of generating new insights into how cities are formed and how new structures emerge, can be used to inform better urban design and urban planning which will be robust and relevant in a way that the plans of the past were not. To take the argument further, we must now turn to real places and see how the new geometry is consistent with urban patterns both within and between cities.

Growing cities

The skeletal structure of the industrial city is tree-like with radial street systems converging on the historic core. As cities grew around this core, they expanded into their hinterland in radial fashion, a little like the hypothetical square city in Figure 6. The street system is itself hierarchical with a few main radials, a larger number of district streets, and many neighbourhood roads. This hierarchy is easily seen in any modern city. In Figure 9 overleaf, we show the street system of the British industrial town of Wolverhampton in the vicinity of its centre. We have colour-coded the system according to the distance from the centre of its retail core. It is fairly clear that this mirrors the way in which Wolverhampton grew, except that in the last 30 years, a ring road has been used to divert traffic from the core. If you look at the radial road structure of the Greater London region, which is at the next scale up from Wolverhampton, the routes converge on the City, and layers of ring road – the North Circular Road, the M25 Orbital Road and so on – have thence been added during this century. The route structure has clear, hierarchical organisation as can be seen in Figure 10, while this picture also shows the fractal nature of the coastline and river estuary east of the metropolis. If we were to zoom in on this structure, we would see radial routes focusing on lesser order centres appearing at every level down, even to the level of the neighbourhood. Interestingly, as traffic focusing on centres has increased, the need to bypass such centres, has grown and a new hierarchy of circumferential

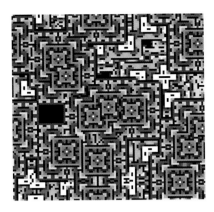
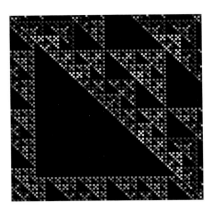

LEFT: Figure 6. Fractal carpets: land use patterns in hypothetical cities; CENTRE: Figure 7. An urban landscape; RIGHT: Figure 8. Sierpinski cities: colonising space with sparse structures

roads – orbitals and beltways – is emerging. The basic pattern of radial routes and the new pattern of orbitals repeats itself through the scales as fractal geometry dictates.

Different types of fractal structure exist in planned street systems particularly at the housing and residential scale. From the 1920s, innovative forms of pedestrian-vehicular segregation where cars and people were separated, were introduced in the Garden Suburbs and the New Towns schemes. At Radburn, New Jersey, in the late 1920s, Henry Wright and Clarence Stein developed such systems where there was a clear hierarchy in terms of local and distributor roads for vehicles, and paths for pedestrians. A schematic of the original plan for Radburn is shown in Figure 11. It is easy to see hierarchical organisation here. This has been replicated in many such housing layouts which are closer to the kinds of hypothetical fractals discussed earlier than are the organic and slowly growing forms that characterise the way most areas in cities develop. In fact, fractal geometry makes no distinction between planned and organically growing forms other than the fact that organically growing forms are often deterministic fractals with some noise or randomness added.

When these tree-like structures are embedded into urban development, we begin to see typical patterns emerge which are clearly fractal. If we also consider population densities, we see how cities begin to fill their space. Figure 12 shows the population density of Greater London where higher to lower densities are illustrated through the yellow to red colour spectrum. The pattern looks tree-like to a certain extent, yet its complexity suggests that it must have been built up not from one seed but from many. Many scales are represented in this pattern, and it can only be represented effectively using processes that build up from the small to the large – in short, processes which scale. The fractal dimension of London in these terms is nearer 2 than 1, while its boundaries which represent another way at looking at space-filling, are nearer 1 than 2. If we were to consider the third dimension, then life gets more difficult. Most of London with the exception of the City, the West End, and parts of the inner area, is largely two-storey residential and overall, it is likely that measuring fractal dimension into this third dimension would yield a dimension close to 2 than 3. Given the number of holes in the two-dimensional map, dimension measured in this way may even

be below 2. However, were we to look at the City, then we might find dimensions greater than 2. In fact we computed the dimension of the Manhattan skyline as 1.56 and a good rule of thumb in fractal geometry is that if the same processes occur in the next dimension up, the fractal dimension would simply be the first one plus 1, in this case $1.56 + 1 = 2.56$. No one to our knowledge has really looked at cities in this way, although readers of *AD* might have expected our fractals to be those in 3D rather than 2D. However, this represents a frontier still to be explored and hopefully, some readers of this article will be encouraged to do this.

There are several ways of building fractal models which generate structures which fill space around some seed which acts a starting point. The most ambitious attempts to date are based on processes of local diffusion such as those found to generate structures such as crystals, electric breakdown, viscous fingers and such-like growth phenomena in physics. Let us refer to one specific technique which we have used extensively to simulate different kinds of fractal city called Diffusion-Limited Aggregation or DLA. This works as follows. Consider a seed which is planted at the centre of a space criss-crossed by a fine lattice and imagine that a series of particles is launched randomly one at a time from a long distance away from the seed. When a seed is launched, it wanders one lattice step at a time in any random direction. If it strays too far (outside the limits of the space), it dissolves or is destroyed and a new particle is launched. If the particle stays within the space, then eventually it will reach the seed and when it does it sticks; a new particle is launched. When this reaches the cluster it, too, sticks, and thus the cluster begins to grow in this manner. What do you think the cluster will look like eventually? Well, it turns out that this simple process generates a growing tree or dendrite around the seed. The reason is that as a particle sticks to a seed, it forms a branch which makes it ever more likely that when particles reach the growing cluster they will stick to already forming branches and avoid the fissures in-between. In fact, they are likely to encounter the branches first, just as if you drop a stone through a tree from above, although there may be many more spaces between branches than space occupied by the branches, the chance of the stone hitting a branch is very high because of the convoluted nature of the branches.

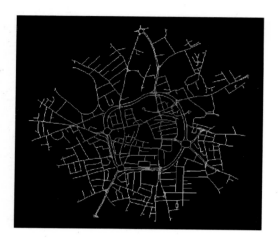

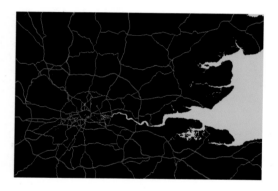

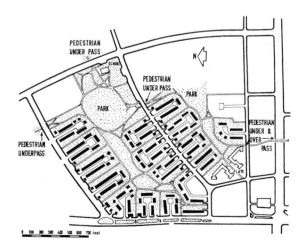

ABOVE: *Figure 9*. Tree-like Wolverhampton; CENTRE: *Figure 10*. Fractal road networks, Greater London; BELOW: *Figure 11*. Hierarchical route segregation, Radburn, New Jersey; OPPOSITE: *Figure 12*. The fractal metropolis: London's population density

We do not have to simulate the structure in this fashion although this is easy enough to do so. A more general version of the model exists in which we can weight the probability that the particle sticks to a growing branch. When this weight is very high, this means that when a branch begins to form, every particle will stick to the tip of the branch and a linear structure will emerge. If the weight is zero, then the particle can stick anywhere and an amorphous mass will form. As we vary the weight from zero to a large number, the structure changes from a 2-dimensional solid mass to a 1-dimensional line. All interesting cases lie between these limits. As the value of the weight falls, the structure becomes more and more dense with its fractal dimension falling from 1 towards 2. Classic dendrites associated with DLA have a dimension of 1.71. In our book *Fractal Cities*, we argue that this is the likely *a priori* dimension for industrial cities, near many of the dimension values we have measured for actual cities. We have generated typical cities using DLA and its generalisation and we show some of these in Figure 13. Our model does in fact have real meaning. To generate a linear city naturally (with a fractal dimension of 1), we have to constrain development so much that we only allow development on the end of what has been developed so far. Thus for any structure that fills space sparsely, we need very tight restrictions such as those used to generate the fractal carpets in Figure 6. As we relax these controls, we generate cities which fill ever more of their space, and when there is no control, everything gets filled, which is what would happen if you had no planning controls whatsoever. Or would it? We doubt it because human behaviour itself provides structure, and thus the ultimate quest of our new science is to find the rules that generate real cities.

Our last examples take urban form to the higher scales, to the region and to the nation. In Figures 14 and 15, we show the fractal structure of the megalopolis centred on south-east England, alongside the urban structure of Great Britain. When we examine the system of cities that form at these scales, it is clear that their number and their frequency as well as their form follow fractal laws which in physics and biology are called scaling laws. These reflect the scale invariance of fractal phenomena; if we were to take away the visual cues from Figures 14 and 15 which are the coastlines and the sea and which lead us to recognise the forms as being part of Britain, then the patterns could be at the same or at any scale down to the most local. London could be a small town while the nation could be the metropolis. At the global level, the distribution of the world population is, of course, also fractal, revealing that for the first time, we have a framework which enables us to link form to function, geometry to geography, space to time, and the present to the past. On this last point, there are now many examples which show how urban structure evolves through space and time and it is becoming clear how fractal structure evolves and changes.

Throughout our discussion, we have emphasised spatial structure, notwithstanding the fact that we have generated these structures through a kind of mathematical time. In Figure 16, we show the growth of the Washington DC-Baltimore metropolis from the late 18th century to the modern day. From this it is clear how fractal structure evolves. Two seeds start the growth which accelerates, eventually fusing the two urban areas as the sprawl gains speed. What the future form of urban society might be is uncertain. Some argue that all places will be urbanised but that fractal laws will still operate at every scale. Within this, there may be transitions to new forms of city which match radically new

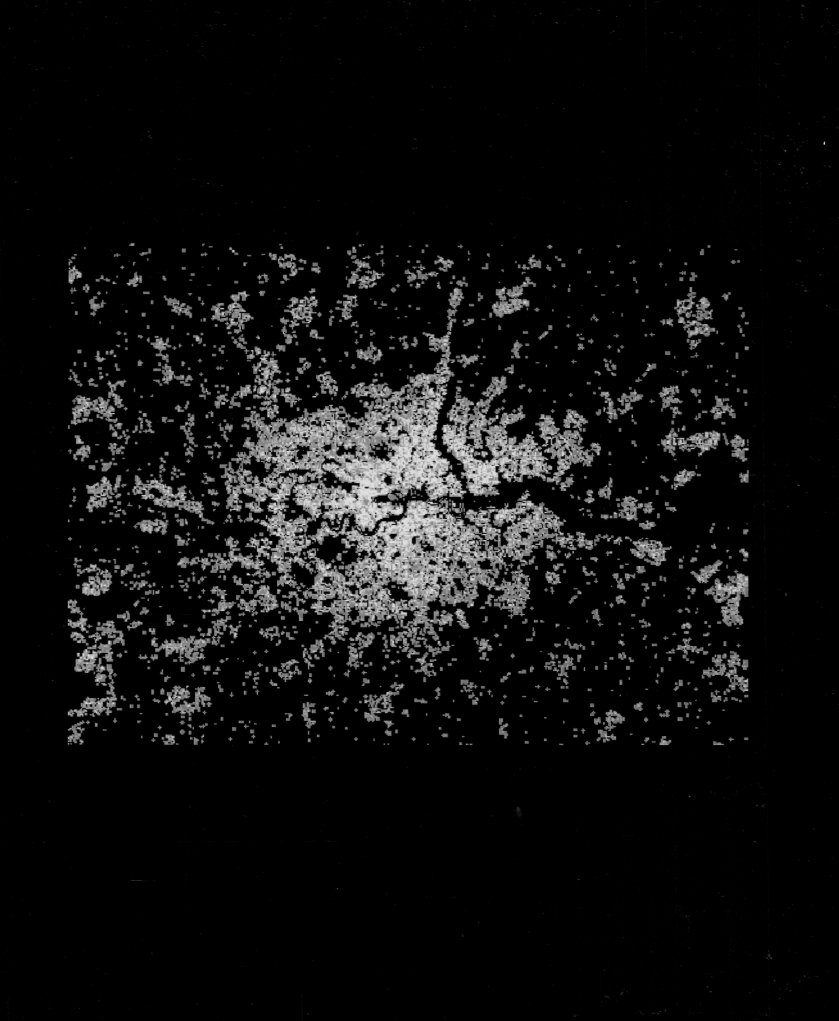

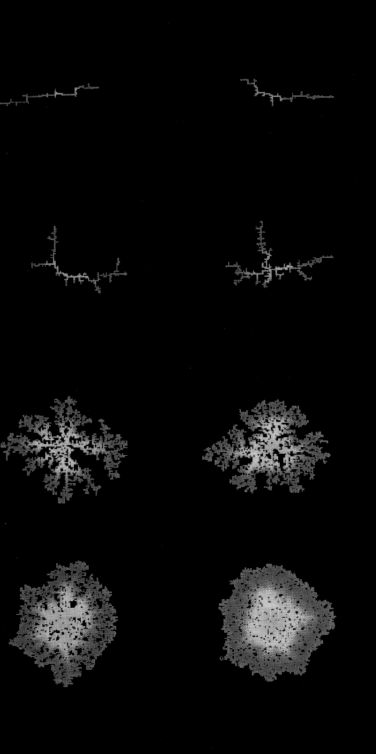

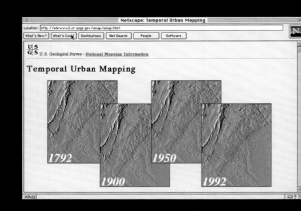

LEFT: *Figure 13*. Simulating urban form: linear to concentric cities;
ABOVE and CENTRE: *Figures 14 and 15*: Fractal Britain and the fractal
structure of the megalopolis, south-east England; BELOW: *Figure 16*.
Urban growth of the Washington-Baltimore metropolis

technologies. But whatever the future, in developing relevant insights about urban form, fractals and its place in the new science will be essential.

Towards a postmodern science of cities

The continuing challenge which has at last begun through these developments in fractal geometry is to link social process to spatial and physical form. This was David Harvey's challenge to urbanists almost a generation ago which dominated his book *Social Justice and the City* published in 1972 (by Edward Arnold, London). In fact Harvey's challenge was issued at the beginning of the long retreat from physicalism into social theory but the new science and the rise of post-modernism marks the beginning of the return. However, it is easier to see fractal form at more aggregate scales, in 2-dimensions rather than 3 and for cities in their entirety rather than in their elements. The real challenge is to build the continuing link through the scales, from the metropolis through the neighbourhood, to the street and the building plot and even beyond into the building itself.

We have no doubt that fractal geometry has much to say at more micro scales but so far, formally structured data has been lacking in this domain and architects have not been exposed sufficiently to the new geometry to be able to see its potential. It would be nice to think that within a decade, work will have begun in developing a fractal geometry for architecture linking form to process, just as there have been developments of shape grammars and cellular automata at these scales already.

The quest to move into higher dimensions is also important. The core of the city could be seen as a sculpted fractal, as a volume that is successively unpacked as well as packed by smaller volumes of different sizes. There is much in the geometry that is suggestive here. Look back at Figure 1 and consider how we might extend all this into the third dimension. With an increasing number of high density city centres being available in digital, solid geometry – CAD – form, the quest to interpret such development through fractals is now feasible. Finally, none of this would be significant were it not for the possibility that we are on the threshold of developing ideas of how fractals are generated, how they evolve. If fractal geometry is the way of linking form to function, the next decade should see new theory emerge which shows how forms and functions co-evolve spontaneously and through design.

Michael Batty is Professor of Spatial Analysis and Planning, Centre for Advanced Spatial Analysis, University College London, 1-19 Torrington Place, London WC1E 6BT, UK (email: m.batty@ucl.ac.uk)

Paul Longley is Professor of Geography, University of Bristol, University Road, Bristol BS8 1SS, UK

Further reading

There are many more examples in our book *Fractal Cities* (Michael Batty and Paul Longley, Academic Press, San Diego, CA, 1994) which provides a systematic introduction to the measurement and simulation of urban structure using fractal geometry but the bible is by Bennoit Mandelbrot, *The Fractal Geometry of Nature* (W H Freeman, San Francisco, CA, 1983), which is a marvellous, esoteric, mindboggling book, well worth delving into time and time again.

A source of great inspiration. Michael Barnsley's *Fractals Everywhere* (Academic Press, San Diego, CA, 1988) is equally arcane, almost inaccessible to non-mathematicians but a wonderful illustration of the power of modern mathematics and a *tour de force* when it comes to methods.

A very readable and cogent introduction to the entire field is Hans Lauwerier's *Fractals: Endlessly Repeated Geometrical Figures* (Princeton University Press, Princeton, NJ, 1991, and Penguin Books, Harmondsworth, Middlesex, UK, 1992).

Applications abound. Physics is full of fractals, as is computer graphics. The various books by Heinz-Otto Peitgen, Harmut Jurgens and Dieter Saupe are worth consulting especially *Fractals for the Classroom: Part 1 and Part 2* (Springer, Berlin, 1992) for these contain many applications to diverse fields and provide a useful overview.

Links between fractals and chaos can be mystical but a good medium is James Gleick's *Chaos: Making a New Science* (Viking, New York, 1987). However, if you want to delve into the essence of chaos, pursue the eminently readable book by the father of chaos, Edward Lorenz's *The Essence of Chaos* (University of Washington Press, Seattle, WA, 1993).

Another readable exposition which links the field to other branches of complexity theory is by Peter Coveney and Roger Highfield, *Frontiers of Complexity* (Faber and Faber, London, 1995).

Finally, let us note some papers. Mandelbrot's 'How Long is the Coast of Britain?', *Science*, Volume 155, pp 636-8, 1967, marks the beginning of the field, while other related applications to cities can be found in Michael Batty, 'Cellular Automata and Urban Form: A Primer', *Journal of the American Planning Association*, 63 (2), pp266-74, 1997, and in journals such as *Environment and Planning B*.

VAN BERKEL & BOS

THE ERASMUS BRIDGE
Rotterdam

The Erasmus Bridge is generated by an intricate system of references to and deviations from surrounding typologies – a system which calls to mind Derrida's term *differance*. While dockside cranes may be recognised in the main shape of the pylon, such meanings are simultaneously subject to undermining by transformations and deviations. The bridge, however, is also a project permeated with the political aspects of the mobile forces. Even more important in this context than the insidious power of its geographical surroundings is the project's large-scale double identity with all its interlocking public and engineering implications.

Although most observers choose to reconstruct the bridge as an intuitive gesture stemming directly from the personality of the architect, this would be simplistic. The mobile forces guiding this project were many and varied; the political aspects involved pertained to those forces most subject to mutability. It says much about the public significance attached to the bridge, long a controversial issue in the city, that when it was the subject of a prize last year, this was awarded to the Rotterdam councillors who had voted in favour of the bridge. The public dimensions of a project with such consequences for a city cannot be denied; yet they go beyond the tactical manoeuvres of the moment.

The primary issue is the deeper, almost hidden political significance of the bridge in the context of the self-image of the city, its history and projected future. It is the energy of the docks, the abrupt 20th-century modernity of architecture and infrastructure, the pragmatism and drive that form the principal constituents of what Rotterdam classifies as its authentic self. These qualities differentiate it from Amsterdam (17th-century classical/atmospheric) and The Hague (administrative/19th-century respectable). And the expectations are that the bridge – the last connection between north and south before the North Sea, and the object of speculation as the presumed attractor of new developments in the Kop van Zuid area – will comply with these images of authenticity.

When these public expectations are related to the rather inaccessible discourse of civil engineering, the contours present themselves as a bridge which, as a synopsis of the desires of the city, distributes its forces resolutely, rationally and in hierarchic poise over the river. That the Erasmus Bridge, on the contrary, displays an asymmetrical balance more fragile than robust, can be ascribed to a rereading of the city in all its undiagnosed complexity, together with an interest in the anti-tradition of civil engineering.

Informing the process of making the Erasmus Bridge is a constantly modulating conflict between the two traditions of bridge building; the rational and the experimental. The existence of these two traditions in civil engineering has been suppressed by the moral rhetoric of the rationalists. They persistently deny the existence of interests other than structural and economic ones, whereby Early Modern design principles are still accorded unconditional validity. It is becoming increasingly clear, however, that in practice the two contrasting traditions modify each other and that the stasis of the rationalist discourse bases its legitimacy on an impossible condition of immutability.

Architecture's contribution consists of blurring further the distinction between the two engineering traditions; for large-scale civil engineering projects, particularly those in urban contexts, are not impervious to architecture. That this civil engineering dispute has 'political' implications which influence the course of the project (taking sides involves being attacked, as the project contested) is a consequence as inexplicit and unacknowledged as it is inevitable. Studying the history of the project clearly shows that one manifestation of this conflict emerged in the preliminary design phase and concerned the placement of the back stays. These were present in the first sketches, but set fairly low; they subsequently disappeared and became the issue at stake in a public sparring match. After further structural studies they returned, though now placed high and close to the pylon so that they rose steeply, while the pylon itself became shorter and more slender.

Only one element remained the same through all these changes, and though permanently visible was hardly remarked upon: this was the horizontal foot of the pylon hugging the slender road deck. The fact that the back stays also connect to this horizontal component meant that the support structure now took the form of a bracket. The high placement of the back stays resulted in a bending moment in the diagonal pylon; this moment was exploited so that the bend could be permanently fixed, which in fact precipitated a new bridge type. Ensuing from this, the construction of the pylon was worked out in greater detail; the ratio between the height of the pylon and the width of the span across the river was reduced from 1:1.5 to 1:2; the width of the pylon was reduced to a mere 3 metres at its narrowest point.

These continual permutations are themselves an important component of the potential countermovement of the bridge. For if we analyse the shifting areas of tension, interplay of forces and events leading up to the Erasmus Bridge project, public response mechanisms and civil engineering defiance are almost impossible to tell apart.

Although it is impossible to isolate one factor that has guided these processes, the surprising importance of the computer drawing in these subordinate activities needs to be acknowledged. The computer offers the architect so much insight into a field once largely beyond his grasp, that he now has a much greater say in engineering projects. At the same time this argument cannot be seen as distinct from other interests; the shared, public space of the computer simulates

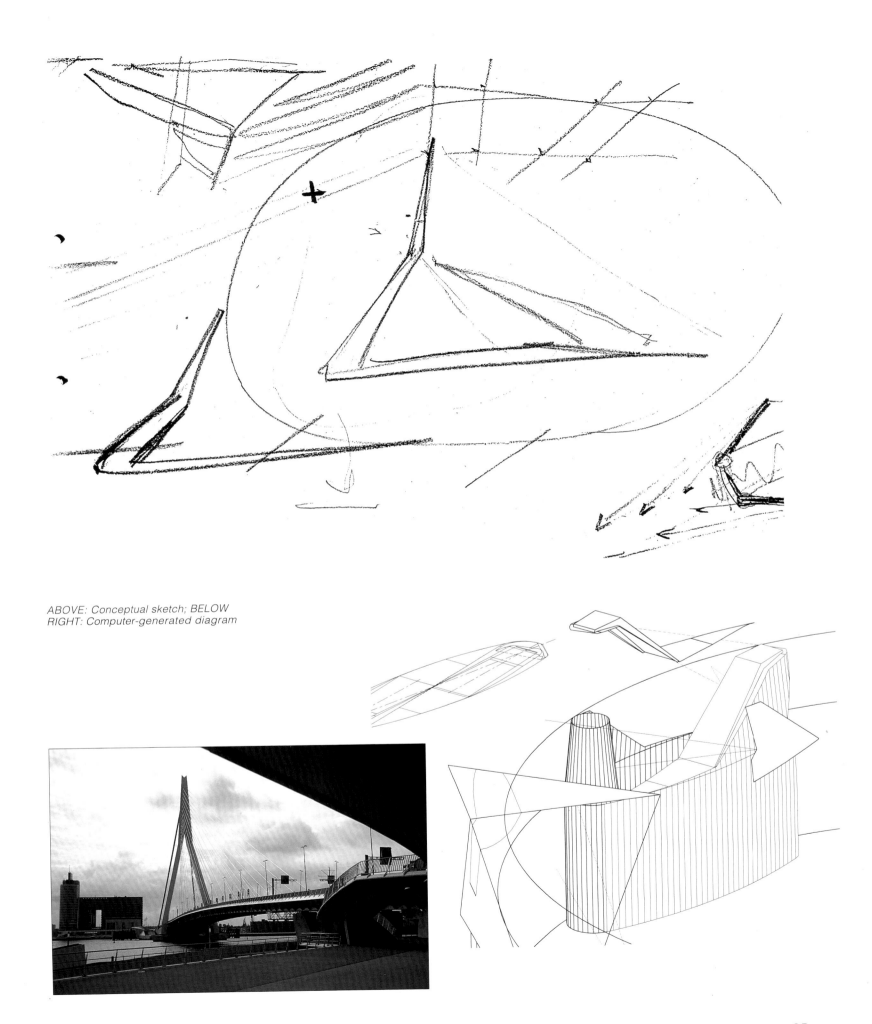

ABOVE: Conceptual sketch; BELOW
RIGHT: Computer-generated diagram

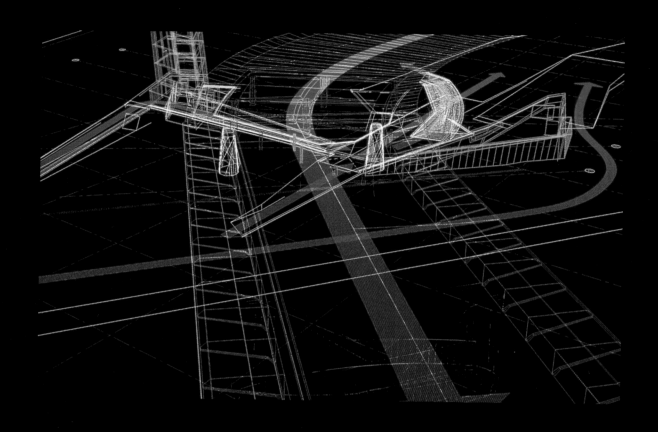

ABOVE: Computer generated perspective;
BELOW: Model

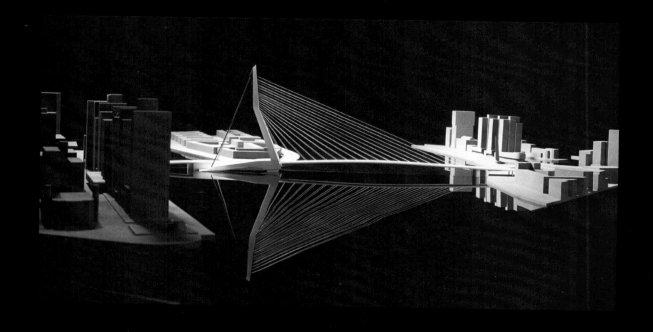

hat of the city, supplementing it with a
new calculated image of urban phenomena. For instance, it provides intensity
graphs in which the bridge emerges as
an urban artefact in a way quite separate
rom every traditional planning discourse.

  What these and other studies demonstrate is a sharpening of the double life of
each extensive urban and infrastructure
object; despite its ineluctable solitary
permanence, in the individual, subjective
xperience it is short-lived, intensive and

massive. The two realities exist concurrently, the bridge being there as a fixed
point in the city and also as a fragmented
series of images of stays, lights, traffic
lanes. Its multiple identity is insurmount-
able at every level. However one approaches the project, ambiguities,
transformations and combinations of
forces keep clamouring to the fore. The
combining of forces at this scale is
continued down to the level of detail by
the bridge's involvement in infrastructural

and urbanist considerations.

  To attribute such manifest asymmetry
to an urban project is probably the
bridge's most provocative aspect. It is
impossible to simply reduce the urban
effect of the bridge to that of a andmark,
for it stems from an extensive programme
at various levels of planning to which no
single architectural gesture is applicable.

Ben van Berkel and Caroline Bos

We make cages out of our structures. We want our buildings to have frameworks but out of a Cartesian compulsion we compartmentalise space into strict horizontals and verticals. Our designs reinvent the topographies of rigid skeleton.

Locked in right angles, the assumption is of order as a rigorous delineation and within that the building as object. So the external boundary is set, and by grid and sub-grid a method of exact subdivisions begins; a diminution into regular, repetitive fixings of space. Within the rigidity nothing moves. Like soldiers on the parade ground everything is at arm's length, the formation of regiment being taken as more important than the individual impulse. The formal is taken as read and a regimental concept of order accepted as the status quo. The imagination is immobilised. We trap movement.

In the static perfection of the modernist cube, with its minimalist palette of glass and transparency, we see right into the emptiness of the container. Structure seems to have no response but to stand mute. In high-tech elaborations we see only the extension of a mechanistic tradition; steel mast and cable, structure as machine. In terms of space and configuration, inspiration seems to have given way to an overpowering technology. But is geometry this artificial wasteland or does it have some kind of animation, allowing the outcome of an intervention in its potential to be guesswork rather than a predestined plot? If there is life to this geometry perhaps we should go forward more cautiously, trading more on intuition, more on instinct than on the assumption of space being neutered, capable only of containerisation.

In the irregular rhythms and diversity we see all around us, the real is highly complex; it is rich in entanglements. So why not look for characteristics that 'seed' the complex and give starting points to an inner logic which could lead outwards to the idea of ensemble and coherence? Traditionally, A relates to B and then B to C in hierarchical connections of formal logic. But could the idea of A into B back into A back into B build on some kind of feedback loop? Why not structure as trace, as episode, as staccato or punctuation? Then as catalyst, the idea of *local* would arise; *juxtaposition* becomes rhythm; *hybrid* entities are taken as natural and positive and not as odd, freaky, or the exception. We enter a general domain of overlap where what is site specific, a a particular instant or viewpoint, may become order. Ambiguities arise, interpretation is the only way forward. There is no single reading of such a building.

The informal

The informal is not random or arbitrary, it relies on overlap to bring forward a series of shifting certainties – its logic is contingent upon initial conditions. Chaos is seen as a succession of several orders, quite different to the idea we have of trapping the arbitrary and calling it order.

The twisting in and out of a Moebius strip is informal. A room that turns to wall and floor, a floor that is skin, where boundary does not mean border, is also part of it. Two columns out of step side by side, of different shapes and material are part of it. Instead of regular formally-controlled measures, varying rhythms and wayward impulses take root. Opportunity is seen to give chance, a chance!

The classical determinism of Newton pictured force as an arrow, straight and true. It bridged the void in unwavering linearity – the fixed link of a rigid chain of logic. Now we see force differently, as a minimum path through a field of potential. Dependent on local conditions that path may vary but the trajectory is based on moments of mutual cooperation, a simultaneous juxtaposition that charts a minimum path.

In the informal there are no distinct rules, no fixed patterns to be copied blindly. If there is a rhythm it is in the hidden

FROM LEFT TO RIGHT: Jussieu University Library, Paris – elevation; unwinding floor slabs; Kunst-hal, Rotterdam, entrance

connections that are inferred and implied but not noticed as obvious. The answers lie in the relationship between events. Hybrid situations are taken as valid starting points and not unfortunate accidents. Two events close together are not seen as exceptional but as a dynamic that sends out particular vibrations.

Structural solutions that arise from the informal impart hidden energies to a building. The connectivity is improvising; the equilibrium put together in ad hoc instants. *The informal acts as an agent of release* and architecture is free from the traditional notions of fixed grid and locked in cage – the topography of such buildings is different.

What is new is the intuitive rational and a new kind of structure.

Recent projects

Several recent projects with Rem Koolhaas incorporate structure as informal response to space. In the case of the library for the Jussieu University of Paris, the release of the vertical bracing from its traditional lines of concentration in a building, to distribute throughout the cross section as a scatter, allowed floors to lift and spiral. Stability was given by a series of local interventions, coupling various discontinuities back to nodes, incorporating the slanting floor elements themselves as bracing elements.

The structure of the Kunst-hal in Rotterdam is full of staccato and off-beat rhythms. Columns move out of regular sequence in a shameless opportunism, to accept conflicts that arise from not ironing out and 'planning' evenness in the roof structures. As a result, the entrance area to the art gallery gains three columns, of different materials and section, whose juxtaposition introduces and defines 'threshold' in a fresh, new way. The horizontal bracing of the roof in the main upper gallery of the museum is a sweeping arc that punctuates the roof beams and begs the question as to what the curving red line in space is for; is it decoration or structure? But does it matter, why should structure be comprehensible and explicit? Structure need not advertise itself. In fact, deep structure will never be seen. The algorithm, or secret pattern of its generators, is the impetus that stays hidden. I prefer structure *as trace rather than skeleton*, with pathways that attempt to interpret space. If the trace is continuous and explicit, well and good, the continuum is celebrated; if fragmentary and intermittent, then the discrete is allowed a say. Borders vanish and boundaries travel in this new paradigm, they become lines of passage and phase points of transition. Limits become thresholds. These are the dynamics of *potential* latent in position, where even a humble point is empowered as the first leap of concretisation out of a supercharged void.

To achieve the great sweep of concave roof in the Lille exhibition and conference centre, I proposed to Koolhaas a hybrid solution of timber and steel using, unusually, timber as tension chord and steel angle tees for compression booms. A simple reinforcement bar bent into a wave form provided the shear bracing connecting top angle tee to bottom timber chord. What could have been a pragmatic industrial roof now became a lively surface of striations; the gigantic underbelly of a great boat. Timber lent warmth to the interior, making the huge space more intimate, more approachable – a mark of the informal.

In the most recent project completed with Koolhaas for a villa in Bordeaux, equilibrium takes a flip from its usual stable configurations. Beam lines 'slip' and stagger, both in plan and vertical elevation, giving release to the solid form so that the idea of enclosure is 'airborne'. The traditional solution of evenly distributed bottom support would have given the configuration of 'table' and a static response. But the Bordeaux villa 'flies', the skewed nature of top hung right support juxtaposed with bottom left cradle support, setting up a precise danger point.

Balance is precarious. It is a knife edge. In the sharp juxtaposition of equilibrium there is shock, a polarising excite-

LEFT AND CENTRE: Kunst-hal, Rotterdam roof brace; RIGHT: Exhibition Centre, Lille

Villa in Bordeaux

ment of safety and risk; of uncertainty and unpredictability. The Bordeaux villa seizes the moment – extemporising space in a show of 'look no hands' structure. Though the main form is dark and strong and concrete, even fortress and bunker like, the villa seems to launch itself into space, the exaggeration of structure and its 'slips' making structure itself vanish. The response is typically part of the informal.

The Victoria & Albert Museum

For the V&A Museum extension, the new entrance building, Daniel Libeskind proposed a 'spiral of history'. Far removed from the 'de-con' labels hurled at it, the form was developed as an evolving trajectory, crisscrossing space, continuous and open ended, spiralling upwards. The approach was entirely holistic.

Classical spiral forms revolve around fixed centring; both logarithmic and Archimedean spirals turn in ever widening orbits fixed by a continuous unwrapping of space. There are no discontinuities, no jerks and no jumps. But the spiral of history is different, it is chaotic – its centre moves, the orbits jump. The resulting trace is one of interlock and overlap.

A radius that moves around a circle, stopping in certain instants, will give an irregular polygon trace if the points at which it stops are connected to each other sequentially. If this radius should increase or decrease during rotation the notion of a spiral is introduced. If the centre begins to shift as well during the revolutions then the trace is of a new kind of spiral, a *chaotic* spiral.

When such a trace is taken as a centre line plan of wall elements, and the zigzag on plan is elevated by a series of height offsets, one in relation to the other; and tilts introduced about these centre lines, then a form such as the V&A takes hold. The overlap of the lines become cross-over points giving necessary bearing to the walls, which take their strength from the interlock. The structure as it were 'builds' on itself, standing free; needing

no internal core or extra brace. Floors act as diaphragms and columns do not penetrate the volumes, giving to the interior spaces a meditative and serene quality. The walls are of concrete, weaving a seamlessness into the twisting structure and at the top, to gain light, the spiral turns into glass.

The materiality of the spiral can be further questioned by the sub-pattern tracing (when is structure seamless or buried network?). If there is tiling on the walls, and the pattern of the tiling is such that its configuration could transfer at some point into structure, then decoration turns into substance. This exciting shift is being investigated with the V&A but to look at this fruitfully, a new kind of tiling was needed, a *fractile*.

The 'structure' of the tiling chosen for the V&A is a generic pattern, a network that grows without scale and absolutes. The growth sets in place regulating self-similarities. In an ever breaking network of rivers and tributaries, rhythms of descent and ascent grow. It is a constant replication that looks similar at every step but never quite repeats in pattern. Only three tiles describe the starting point for this adventure but each is derived from the other, setting up an interdependency and intimacy from the outset. The great surprise is that this delicate labyrinth builds on a hidden ancient geometry, that of the golden section!

It is quite astonishing how at the heart of something seemingly open-ended with simultaneous bifurcations at all levels, untamed and wholly modern in concept, there should be this classical mark of perfect ratio. However, there was nothing static about the early classical paradigms: the Greek spirit thrived on relative ideas such as 'interval' and 'proportion', and like Zeno delighted in paradox – not for those early masters the absolute fix of dimension. Classical perfection was taken as a march of several orders, interdependent and bound, one within the other. Algorithm governed; a symphonic geometry went to work to promote and proportion space.

90

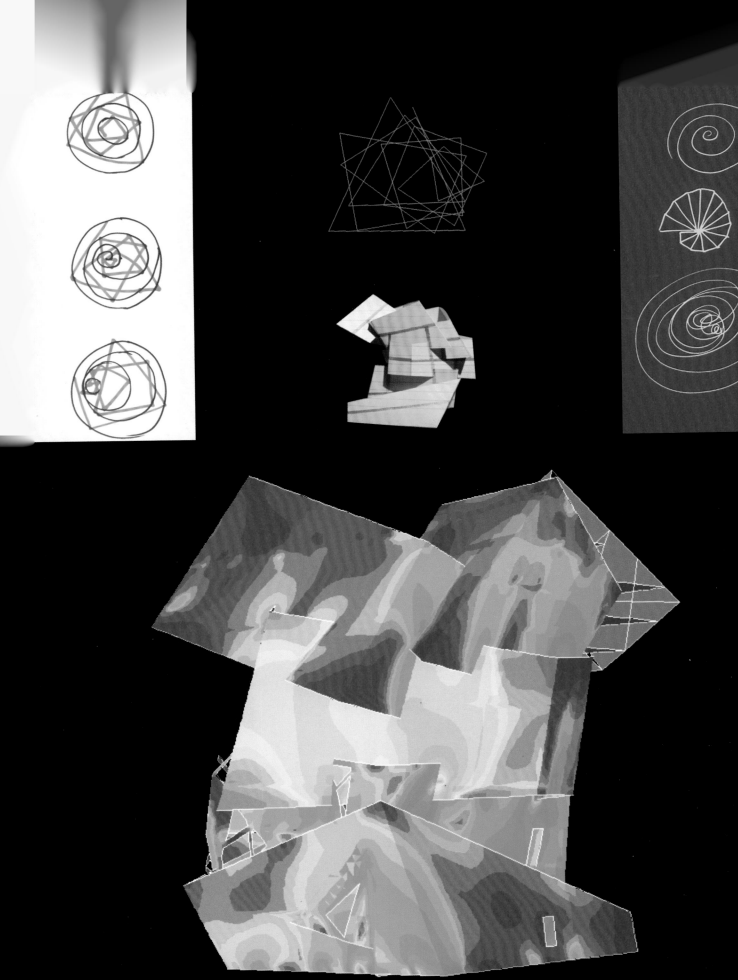

ABOVE LEFT AND RIGHT: Algorithm for chaotic spiral; logarithmic,
Archimedean and chaotic spiral; CENTRE, FROM ABOVE: Plan trace
of walls; working model, V&A; structural analysis, V&A

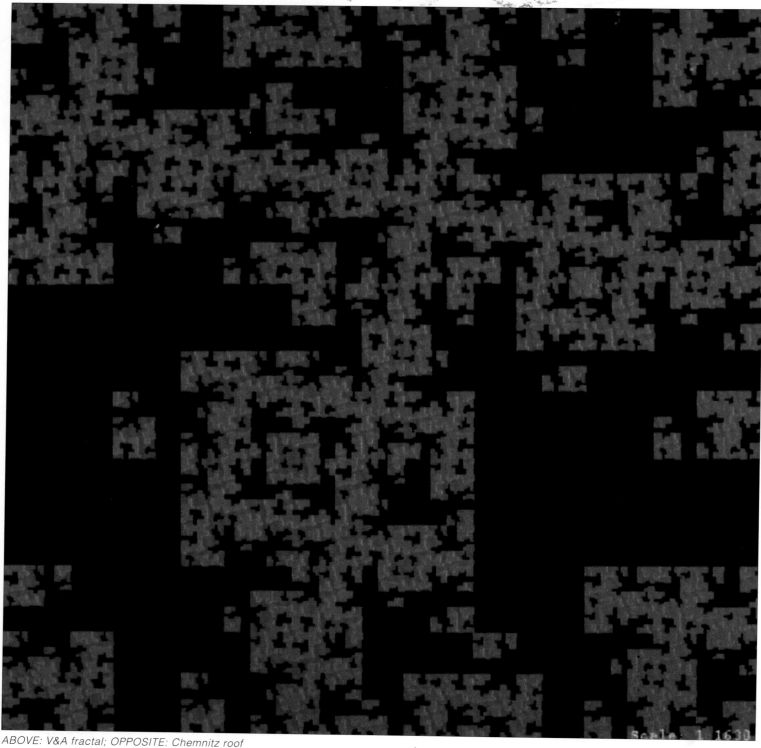

Scale 1:1630

ABOVE: V&A fractal; OPPOSITE: Chemnitz roof

Chemnitz

Stadia designs follow concentric thinking. Typically, a slice is first solved with a cantilever roof coupled to seating stands, and then the cross section is spun round; faithfully following the running track in the idea of extrusion.

Architects Peter Kulka and Ulrich Konig wanted to break this mould in their design for Chemnitz, near Leipzig. They proposed a roof that was uncoupled instead from the stands; one that would not just follow the running track but would cover the whole site. It was a conceptual breakthrough. The uncoupling gave unlimited freedom with the roof acting as some sort of cloud floating over the seating. The randomness of nature, as forest,

was to be brought into the idea of the supporting columns, and the roof, main tier seating, and running track were to be given different orbits, spinning with different outlines and energies – as unpredictable as the games themselves with the outcome of win or lose.

A model was built out of paper to explore the free contours of such open thinking. The result was an extraordinary, longitudinal strip wave form. However, it seemed impossible to impose the logic of transverse, fixed radial cantilevers on such a proposal, and the question was how to respond with 'structure'? Something new was needed, an inner logic with which one could construct an argument.

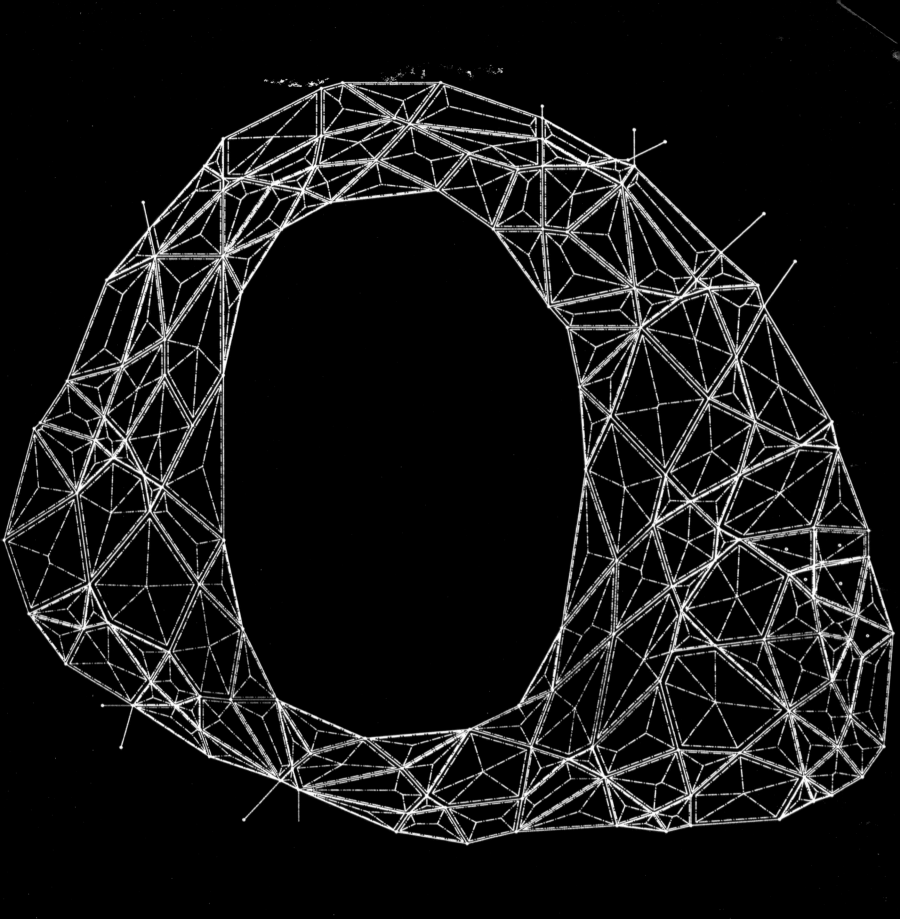

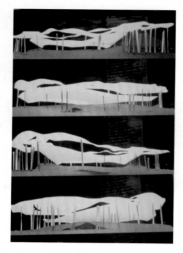
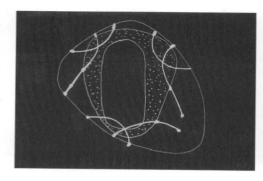
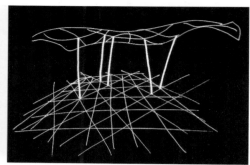

ABOVE L TO R: Chemnitz working model; ring concept; random columns; BELOW: Chemnitz model

The answer arose from three local conditions. On plan, at three places, the back of the seating coincided with the site boundary. There was no available backspan for a traditional cantilever. Instead, three torsion rings were proposed, launching into space. In support of these rings, further rings vaulted into space and an assembly grew, each ring interacting with the other. A steel net formed. To create a rippled form for the roof, the rings were pushed up by a negative gravity on one side and allowed to sag naturally on the other; providing a longitudinal wave form. From the rings, sub-assemblies of structure could be supported to fix the roof cladding in a variety of ways. The openness of the rings offered many possibilities to generate this secondary layer and propose different contours and materials for the external skin.

In relation to the columns, the question was how to gain a notion of the random from pragmatic buildability concerns? In the event the answer was simple; a grid, on the ground, was duplicated and rotated. From the intersection point of the rings on the roof, support lines could now be dropped to the nearest available nodes on the ground. The final pattern of connection would seemingly be random. Thus the columns took root, inclined in different directions, giving density in certain areas or standing alone and isolated as single punctuations elsewhere.

What was a fantasy to start with – the free-form paper model – found an interior logic that built outwards, with rings and rotations of grids, to articulate the many freedoms of the solution. The strategies were wholly part of the informal.

At the competition stage the location of the structural rings was guided by the eye. I was intrigued, though, to see if intuition had any rationale to it; could the patterns of the roof net itself be derived by other means? Did chaos, in the mathematical sense of deterministic algorithm, have anything to do with it; could differ-ent outcomes arise from different start points? In other words, could the roof pattern be self-generated by a chaotic rule? The answer lay in a rotating disc.

Rotating disc

Imagine a black disc in a darkened room. Make a few holes in the disc; shine a light through the holes. Let the disc rotate, and track the light; and travelling waves in the geometry of overlapping cycloids emerge. As the holes vary in position the trace breaks down into a wild scatter or it comes out symmetrical and even. If a further complexity is added and the discs expand and contract, rolling tangential to set contours between a site boundary on one hand and a fixed running track edge on the other, then a net of rings forms. If the disc runs round and round, the 'weave' thickens and grows. An infinity of solutions is possible. Some weaves look like cane work, others give rainbow symmetries, some look like reef coral. Different traces suggest different objects. The results jump scale. Pattern governs the interpretation.

Various properties can now be given to the strands and parameters stitched in to seed 'intelligence' into the overlapping interactions. What looks so free is actually held together by internal strategies. There is a curious 'understructure' to the ensemble and though we read 'free form' something else is felt: a sense of 'nature' and of 'order'.

Chemnitz incorporates all parts of the informal. It is a stadium far removed from traditional encirclings and the focus upon just one fixed revolution. Instead, in the Chemnitz project several revolutions take place and, not least, the one that embraces new structure as informal event.

OPPOSITE, FROM ABOVE: Algorithm for rings; symmetrical trace; chaotic trace; rings from algorithm

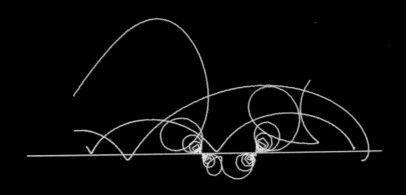

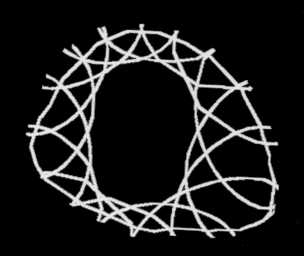

...e is a dynamic. Enquiring into form and configura-
...st principles it admits into the solution the complex as
...New structure takes overlap and ambiguity as a basis for
...gn and the stringent notion of order along Cartesian tramlines
...iscounted – a methodology that is taken as fixed, reductionist,
...and ultimately limiting in scope.

New structure animates geometry. It reawakens an original inspiration of form, enquiring of space itself as to its nature and interpretation. In this scenario buildings become rhythm and sequence and clash and confrontation; if symmetry is there it is in the active coming together of separate tendencies, in balance for only one moment. The traditional pursuit of external object cut by dissecting and unthinking subdividing grid is rejected. Instead, an holistic approach is taken of inner logic informing the whole. The imperative is in-to-out.

In the name of modernism, a final stripping down and denuding of form has taken place and 'structure' relegated to mute submission. The result is a giving up of thought to blankness and transparency, glass and steel – evaporating substance and left-over cage; there is nowhere else left to go. Reductionism has reached its dead end. Design has deconstructed, and minimalism has become a reward label.

Twisted shameless multiplications of surface or texture of form are nowhere to be found. The desire is to conform and offer up constructions in orthodox containers, without the fun of elaborations – no syncopated rhythms, and none of the 'irrational' and spontaneous. Why not a new multiplicity, the idea of a new gothic or romantic?

New science

Surprisingly, new science offers a fresh start.

Rejecting the linear and hand-me-down logic of a top-down hierarchical thinking, new science openly embraces the complex. The nonlinear is adopted. What is new is the admittance of feedback as motive. There is overlap, and the simultaneous is empowered. Incredibly, such starting points of the chaotic are seen to lead towards stabilities and coherence, driven by internal self organising wills. The paradigm is one of emergence, a gathering together of disparate tendencies that move towards one expression of separate wills. Flying in the face of conventional ideas of pre-arrangement, new science proposes the plan instead as the starting point, and the resulting boundary as surprise. Order is only a transient part of the picture, on the edge of turbulence. Somehow able to come together by internal improvisations, order in the sense of organisation and coherence is seen as a safe bet – arising out of the chaotic and unpredictable. Such ideas fly in the face of entropy and the permanent run down holy-grailed into us by the second law of thermodynamics. But then creativity has always been a surprise!

The world is complex and it shifts gear and jumps. We shy away from this difficulty because the mind has to bend round corners and the mathematics is difficult. But the power of modern computing is unleashing what was never before thought possible; we do not have to think anymore along tramlines or be contained to derived notions of linearity. There is a richness out there – we should delight in it. We should explore it.

The fallacy of a reductionist science has been to make us think that the whole can be cut into bits and then reduced down to one final bit – but something always gets lost on the surface of that cutting or splitting knife. Physics has taken us into this atomic and monadic world and now we find that reality blurs, and certainty, chameleon like, transforms into doubt. Is a particle a wave or is it the other way round? Is matter itself a particular vibration of overlapping multidimensional 'strings' or a quantum jump out of the virtual?

The shadowy and the fantastic seem to be the new realities; virtual and nascent, rather than fixed and concrete. We want to understand, make linear relays and logical chains out of the complex, but in trying to remove uncertainty we remove the invisible glue that holds things together. Inevitably something gets lost.

Mathematics is racing forward with nonlinear dynamics high on the agenda. Given a starting point or initial sequence, improvisation and internal rhythms are calculated to lead to coherence. Economic crashes and heart attacks are explained. Research into quasi-crystals and amorphous forms question our hard fixed notions of boundary and structure. Biology is in the vanguard of the new science; chemistry and the other disciplines follow. Where is architecture?

New science = new architecture?

The current investigations and research of the new sciences is based on dynamic living systems. How then does it relate to architecture, built out of fixed forms and static structures? One to one translation of the new science to a new architecture does not seem to be realistic – it only leads to mimicry. Copying nature or chaos ends up looking forced. What is more interesting is to look into the basis of the paradigm that embraces 'risk', and the building up of internal processes that throw up conflict and clash. Ambiguities will arise, such a building will give separate readings due to overlap. One has to interpret as opposed to assume a preconcept.

Does it matter? Why not go on planning containers and repeating equalities and subscribing to static, fixed, ideals of symmetry?

I propose that more than the eye sees the body senses. In response to new structure we may find in the configuration of such network a deeper resonance than the superficial visual. Out of chaos we came; within us is a derived sense of order, not linear and logical, but odd and complex. Responding with one's instinct to raise ancient spells is important – sharpening one's intuition to investigate the runes of form a necessary act. Gaining an insight is important.

Conclusion

There are no fixed rules for new structure, the informal takes care of that. If there is a set rhythm it is in the hidden connections that are implied and felt but not seen, leading to the skewed and oblique or towards the regular and symmetric – it all depends on where one starts.

There is no one reading of such designs – ambiguity forces interpretation. Juxtaposition and hybrid situations are valid and not unfortunate accidents; on a small and intimate scale local actions are trusted to spread outwards and inform the whole. At some point coherence is reached and an 'object' defined. Order, in this sense, is a travelling transient. The method is informal, the framework is new structure. The inspiration is new science.